T0113373

The Anti-social Family

The Anti-social Family

MICHÈLE BARRETT
and
MARY McINTOSH

Second Edition

VERSO

London · New York

First published by Verso 1982
Reprinted 1984, 1985, 1987, 1990
Second edition with new postscript published 1991
© Michèle Barrett and Mary McIntosh 1982, 1991
All rights reserved

Verso
UK: 6 Meard Street, London W1V 3HR
USA: 29 West 35th Street, New York, NY 10001–2291

Verso is the imprint of New Left Books

British Library Cataloguing in Publication Data
Barrett, Michèle, *1949–*
    The anti-social family.—Revised ed.
    I. Title   II. McIntosh, Mary, *1936–*
306.85

ISBN 978-0-86091-545-4

Library of Congress Cataloging-in-Publication Data
Barrett, Michèle.
    The anti-social family/Michèle Barrett, Mary McIntosh.—Rev.
ed., 2nd ed.
        p.   cm.
    Includes index.

    1. Family. 2. Ideology. 3. Sex role. 4. Family policy.
    5. Family policy—Great Britain. I. McIntosh, Mary, 1936—
    II. Title.
    HQ734.B254   1991
    306.85—dc20

Typeset in Monophoto Times New Roman by Servis Filmsetting Ltd,
Manchester
Printed in Great Britain by Dotesios Ltd.

Contents

Preface and Acknowledgements

Marx and Engels may have called, in the polemical rhetoric of the *Communist Manifesto*, for the abolition of the family, but most socialists have long since regarded this as a flight of utopian fancy. An uneasy truce prevails over this most unpopular of orthodox socialist demands. From time to time, however, the calm is troubled, for the politics of the family simply will not lie down. The early years of women's liberation saw a damning indictment of family life; more recently the left has had to confront the equally militant pro-family stance of the new right. We believe that in the long term socialists and feminists must develop a political consensus on the family and that the precondition for this is more open debate on where we stand.

A major difficulty with this is the fact that 'the family' is such a slippery phenomenon. The view we take in this book is that 'the family' must be understood in two senses. It is, of course, a social and economic institution. In the present period it is an institution in which, by and large, households are assumed to be organized on the basis of close kinship relations. We could go further and say that in the present period it is an institution in which households are assumed to be organized, by and large, on the basis of a division of labour between a primary breadwinner (male) and a primary childrearer (female). Although these are *assumptions*, they are nonetheless part of the family, since they form a crucial element of the conditions on which women and men are employed, the level of their wages, and state taxes and benefits.

Many feminists have pointed out that as a social institution this form of family-household is markedly less prevalent than it is usually assumed to be. The stereotypical nuclear family accounts, roughly, for only a third of households in Britain today. Yet the media give the impression that the entire population is securely bound up in it. So a second dimension of what we refer to when we talk about 'the family' must be the family as an ideology. In many ways the institution and the ideology are reciprocally related, enjoying mutual reinforcement. Yet the ideology of the family is perhaps much stronger, in its own right, than we often allow. The model of family life has pervaded our society in its public institutions to such an extent that, far from speaking of the decline of the family, we should be speaking of the familial character of society.

It is this twofold character of 'the family' that makes it particularly difficult to analyse. Certainly it accounts for the strategy we have had to adopt in writing this book, where different chapters focus on what inevitably appear to be quite disparate topics and levels of analysis. The family can be addressed from the point of view of what needs it is thought to serve; how it is represented culturally; how one understands the acquisition of femininity and masculinity; what should be done about state policy and the law. Clearly some of the issues discussed can more readily be translated into 'strategies for change' than others. Our final chapter sets out for discussion some possibilities of a practical kind. These are not necessarily the most important changes to fight for, and certainly not the only ones, but we regard them as possible concrete targets. More general changes, such as the total eradication of familial ideology from the media and all public discourse, can readily be inferred from the book's general discussion.

Two notable absences from the book need some brief explanation. We do not make it clear whether the analysis we present applies across the several family forms of the different ethnic groups in Britain or is restricted to the dominant 'white' family. The appeal of these different family forms, and their constraints and tensions, are undoubtedly distinct, the more so because they exist as forms of ethnic solidarity in a hostile environment. Nevertheless we believe that the same principles of critique would apply, though it is not for white feminists to work out the detailed form that these would take. Some of the strategies for change that we propose would open up new opportunities for everyone in the society, whatever their ethnic origin.

A second absence concerns the relation between the family and sexual preference. It would be ironic for us to be accused of reproducing the hegemonic heterosexism of our culture. Nevertheless we have to some extent inevitably done this, as we believe the present ideology of the family to be so steeped in heterosexism that any realistic engagement with familialism must locate the discussion within that framework.

We have found this a difficult book to write and for this reason are particularly grateful to those who have helped us. Francis Mulhern gave considerable advice and encouragement, and Catherine Hall commented on the entire draft for us. We also thank David Plotke for information about the American pro-family lobby, and Angela Weir for comments on chapter 4. Obvious though it may be, we should point out that many of the ideas of the book are indebted to discussions and campaigns in the women's movement; in particular we have benefited greatly from the work of Rights of Women and of the 'Fifth Demand' (legal and financial independence) group, especially in relation to policy recommendations.

It is not hard to identify the reason why the book has been difficult to write. The family is a contentious and emotive subject and we are painfully aware that many of our own family and friends will disagree with the arguments we make here. Although we have used a rather impersonal style, no author or reader can be completely detached from the personal implications of the arguments. But personal life is at one and the same time the story of our own lived experiences – the context of our deepest motivations, rewards and frustrations – and also the product of a particular moment in history and a particular structure of society. So we are often divided between subjective experience on the one hand and political analysis on the other. In recognizing the powerful appeal of the family, and acknowledging the real satisfactions that it can offer, we have drawn from our own experiences. We hope that the book contributes to the difficult project of reconciling private experience and social need, and of dealing with the ambivalence and contradiction that bedevil the political theorization of subjectivity.

I

A Question of Values

1. The Political Context

The family has long been a controversial subject but the
present political conflict over it is one in which the stakes have
been raised significantly. Indeed, a delegate to the Council of
Europe in Strasbourg, speaking of the 'paganistic and atheis-
tic' practice of artificial insemination, fearlessly identified
nothing less than 'a world campaign to undermine marriage
and the family as the fundamental unit of society'.[1] If such an
international conspiracy does exist, systematically struggling
to erode the integrity of the family, it is certainly meeting a
vigorous fightback.

The European Parliament is a case in point. At present it is
developing a policy on the family, with the intention of
supporting this institution in all member states. The papers
provided as background information for the debate on these
resolutions are singularly alarmist in tone and differ sharply
from the position in favour of equality officially taken by the
EEC. Mrs M.L. Cassanmagnago Cerretti gives a lengthy dis-
quisition on the parlous state we are now in: 'It is striking that
the widespread disintegration of the concept of the family as
the nucleus of society, the increasing instability in family
relationships reflected by the spread of cohabitation and
divorces, *the new position of women in society and their wish to
work*, the crisis in traditional moral values, the falling birth

[1] *Gay News*, 227, October 1981, p. 7.

rate, which is now approaching or even falling below the rate required for the population to renew itself, are trends common to all the countries of Europe, even if they vary in intensity. Thus the future and the very survival of these countries are at risk.' One of the many proposals put forward is to increase contact with 'the various European family associations', so that policy can be more responsive to 'the grass roots'.[2]

In Britain the family has become a political football – so Jean Coussins and Anna Coote have described the unseemly spectacle of Labour and Conservative politicians competing for the claim to represent the interests of the family.[3] This suggests that the politics of the family under the Thatcher government are more complex than is sometimes thought. There are, of course, instances such as the now notorious remark by a government minister, Patrick Jenkin, to the effect that had God intended equality he would not have created men and women. It is also true that 'Thatcherism' encodes the ideology that families – for which read 'women' – should be responsible for the day-to-day care of the young, the elderly, the sick and the disabled wherever possible. Welfare cuts of various kinds have increased the domestic burdens of women, who are also particularly vulnerable to unemployment. The policies of the present government, as well as many of its statements, endorse the view that the family should be a self-sufficient enterprise needing little support from the state.

To some extent, however, this familism is part of a broader political rhetoric; it is a metaphor to endow the government's economic policies with a spurious 'commonsense' legitimacy. The chancellor of the exchequer, like any housewife or corner grocer, must balance his books and cannot afford your nursery or hospital. The ideological significance of the metaphor is considerable, but the continual evocation of the family in Thatcher's pronouncements does not mean that the government is pursuing a straightforward policy of 'getting women back into the home'. Class interests, and the class character of

[2] European Parliament, Committee on Social Affairs and Employment, Working Document PE 70:147 'Family Policy in the EEC' (our emphasis).
[3] NCCL/CPAG, *The Family in the Firing Line*, London 1981.

these policies, necessarily render their effects on women complex. At one level, women workers are simply too useful, especially in a situation of deskilling and erosion of wage levels, to be dispensed with. At another, many of the government's tax proposals are explicitly designed to benefit higher-paid women, in line with their overall regressive character. At a third, the prime minister's personal comments on rape and sexual violence – to the effect that women should feel safe on the streets – provide a somewhat surprising inflection to the standard law-and-order position. These few examples all suggest a new set of considerations, as well as the predictable ones, on the politics of the family in contemporary Britain. Against those who argue that 'Thatcherism' takes a straightforward pro-family and anti-feminist stance, it can be pointed out that the position taken is in many ways far more contradictory than the support for a stereotypical nuclear family embedded in the Beveridge Report and the host of welfare policies and reforms developed in the post-war decades.[4]

Although a traditional defence of family values has been boosted by Thatcherism, there is no sense in which a distinct and consistent line is being pursued. Certainly it is hard to argue that the Labour Party offers a very different position on the family. Many of the demands of the poverty lobby are couched in a distinctively familist terminology, and the lobby receives considerable support from reformers on both sides. In this sense political dispute over the family is considerably less sharp in Britain than it has become in the United States, where issues of family and sexual politics have a very high profile in public debate.

It is not necessary for us to recapitulate here the much more explicit and combative position of 'Reaganism' on these questions. Socialists and feminists in the USA have struggled hopelessly against a wave of reaction, moralism and born-again Christianity that has, for example, attacked the right to abortion (and the actual clinics with violence) and reduced

---

[4] See Elizabeth Wilson, *Women and the Welfare State*, London 1977.

funding for it. Anti-homosexual movements have developed popular support and won some disturbing victories. These form part of an explicitly and militantly familist attack by the American 'new right' on the freedoms and rights won by women's and gay movements.

Far more significant than this, however, is the response this wave of familism has generated in sections of the American *left*. An early casualty was support for the unequivocal right to abortion. The publication, in the socialist paper *In These Times*, of a '*debate*' about abortion provoked a vigorous response from feminists and others who argued that ITT had demonstrated 'once again the tenuousness of the socialist commitment to women's liberation', in this instance by its 'disregard for one of the most fundamental and *non-negotiable* demands of contemporary socialist-feminism – free and equal access for every woman to control her own body'.[5] Nevertheless the paper *had* constructed the question of abortion as a 'debate' in which both sides were given credibility as socialist positions.[6] Features in the US press reveal the extent to which an anti-choice position on abortion has gained credibility on the left and among 'progressives', even to the point (at which many right-wing anti-abortionists back down) of denying the right to abortion to women who are the victims of rape or incest.[7]

Abortion is, if you like, an indexical issue. It can provide a litmus test of how well – to put it crudely – feminist and socialist views are bearing up against religious and familist forces. The feminist position on abortion is a woman's right to *choose*, and feminists would defend to the hilt the right of any woman *not* to have an abortion irrespective of the grounds she gave for

---

[5] Judy Stacey and others, *In These Times*, 4 April 1980, p. 15.

[6] The editors stated that 'many of those who oppose abortion rights do so out of genuine religious or moral concern for the sanctity of life. Socialists share their concern and respect their pro-life convictions.' What was particularly offensive was that a committed anti-abortionist used, for the *ITT* readership, an instrumental argument that abortion tended to be used against underprivileged women. See 'Does Free Abortion Hurt the Poor and Minorities?', *In These Times*, 28 February 1980.

[7] 'Why Young Progressives Join the Right to Life Movement', *Tribune*, 15 October 1980, p. A–17.

making this choice. The anti-abortion position is in fact an anti-choice position, imposing, or attempting to impose, particular beliefs on all women.

Underlying the abortion issue is the much broader question of how socialists should respond to the revival of familism. In the USA there has developed a lobby within the left arguing that socialists must put forward *their own* view of the family rather than attack it as an oppressive institution. Such an argument takes as given the enormous popular support for the family – indeed endorses the family as the site of altruism and progressive relationships – and insists that the left has a better claim than the right to 'really' represent family values. This view is most clearly elaborated in a document produced to explain the founding of an organization called 'Friends of the Family'.[8] The authors – Lerner, Zoloth and Riles – believe that the launch of this organization can be presented in the media as a progressive appropriation of familism. They argue that the problems experienced in personal and family life are really the product of alienated work and the competitive market-place. They see support for the family as support for a better life, and – since socialism obviously does offer a better life – see a natural sympathy between socialism and a pro-family position. The thrust of the argument is to make socialist ideas (such as 'humanize the workplace') more popular – or rather, to make apparent the underlying progressive character of popular familist ideologies. Predictably, the protagonists of Friends of the Family are extremely respectful of the religious revival and also incipiently anti-feminist.[9]

What is most odd about this position is that it rests on a very vague identification of the family with personal relations: 'wherever people are making the kind of long-term emotional

[8] Michael Lerner, Laurie Zoloth and Wilson Riles Jnr, 'Bringing it All Back Home: a Strategy to Deal with the Right' Mimeo. Friends of the Family, Oakland, California.

[9] 'Even in the constituencies of religious organizations who have aligned themselves with the New Right there are many moral and righteous people whose religious vision would actually lead them to a more progressive politics if the caricatures about what progressives really stand for could be gotten through' (p. 8). They regard 'the continued legacy of male chauvinism' as a compensation for alienation at work (p. 13).

and financial commitment to each other to take care of each other and provide ongoing love and intimacy we have the development of a family arrangement.'[10] Everything from single-parent families to gay marriages is a family, and so all social issues can be presented in relation to 'the family'. It is not very nice for a family to have its house burgled, so crime is a problem for families; plant closures have unfortunate effects on families; families can be destroyed by sickness and death, so we need a better health system. It appears not to occur to these authors that such events have unfortuate consequences for single people too. The argument panders to popular support for the family by simply declaring that however the family is defined it stands for progressive human values. There have been incisive critiques of the position taken by Michael Lerner and others,[11] but it is a symptom of the left's failure to develop a socialist position on the family that such sloppy and reactionary views even arouse any interest.

Feminism, too, has seen some disturbing responses to the pro-family movement in the USA. One notable example is the latest reflections of Betty Friedan, much discussed in the light of the prominent role she played in the development of feminism in America. She argues that the battle for the Equal Rights Amendment to the American constitution has been lost because of the identification of feminism with an anti-family position and the contamination of feminist politics with issues of abortion and homosexual rights, which she regards as a 'red herring'. Friedan comments that the way in which feminists handled abortion implied a 'lack of reverence for life', and she reminds us that most women are very committed to the family. She argues that 'family' has become a 'buzz word for reactionaries', but that it is really 'the symbol of that last area where one had any hope of control over one's destiny, of meeting one's most basic human needs, of nourishing that core of personhood threatened by vast impersonal institutions and

---

[10] Ibid, p. 13.
[11] See Kate Ellis, 'Can the Left Defend a Fantasized Family?', for the best of these. *In These Times*, 9 December 1981, p. 17.

uncontrollable corporate and government bureaucracies.'[12]
(Shades, here, of Christopher Lasch, whose work we discuss in
detail later on.) Friedan concludes that the 'second stage' of
feminism will be one where we work with men and not against
them; indeed we will be forging alliances with men from
'unions, church and corporation' and 'embracing the family in
new terms of equality and diversity'.
Such ideas are clearly far from accepted in socialist and
feminist circles in the USA. But it remains disturbing that they
are so publicized in the media, and they have led to discussion
and controversy among radicals. We refer to them here not to
draw a complacent distinction between Britain and America.
We believe that positions as reactionary as these would secure
less support, even less interest, on the left here than they have in
the USA. However, this is not because socialist-feminism in
Britain has developed a credible political alternative that
commands the assent of the left, but simply because we have
not had to contend with a massive wave of popular familist
politics on the scale that has assaulted socialists and feminists
in the USA.
Linda Gordon and Allen Hunter, in their interesting discussion of the 'new right', identify some of the reasons why the left
has failed to respond adequately to the situation. They write:
'Socialists have . . . neglected sex and family issues on the
grounds that working class people *as a class* have conservative
views on these issues. We do not accept this evaluation for two
reasons. First, it is time socialists stopped imagining a working
class composed of white patriarchs. Second, we see no reason
why socialists should be more willing to compromise on, say,
women's rights than on any number of currently unpopular
socialist principles.'[13] The comment, and the criticism, would
be equally applicable to the British left. In fact, neither the
socialist nor the feminist tradition has yet developed the
political consensus on the family that we would need in order to

[12] *The Second Stage*, New York 1981.
[13] *Sex, Family and the New Right: Anti-feminism as a Political Force*, Somerville,
Mass., n.d., p. 10 (reprinted from *Radical America*, November 1977 – February 1978).

pursue a struggle with the right. It is widely thought that feminism and socialism are united in a mindless and heartless call for the abolition of the family. Those who, from various political perspectives, object to this demand share a tendency to exaggerate considerably the degree of consensus on this matter in either feminist or socialist thought. There certainly has been a tradition of radical critique of the family on the left, but it is a far more contentious and divisive issue than defenders of the family recognize. It is, in fact, only in the now marginal traditions of utopian, libertarian and anarchist socialism that any full-blown attack on the family can be found. It is hard to argue that the iconoclastic anarcho-feminist views of Emma Goldmann have ever enjoyed universal credibility on the left. Although Marx and Lenin made some polemical gains from a critique of the bourgeois family, it cannot be said that scientific socialism has developed a thoroughgoing rejection of family life as such. Indeed all the main writers on this topic – Marx, Engels, Bebel, Lenin, Trotsky, Zetkin and Kollontai – more or less imply that when women are engaged in wage labour on equal terms with men, and when housework has been socialized, we shall have arrived at the nirvana of proletarian heterosexual serial monogamy. Of course many elements of this socialist critique of the bourgeois family were, and remain, extremely progressive. The insistence that sexuality must be freed from women's financial dependence, argued by Engels and largely accepted in the Marxist-Leninist tradition, is a major step forward, as is Lenin's recognition that domestic labour must be socialized. We do not wish to underplay the progressive character of these demands. But they fall short of an adequate critique of the family, principally in that they fail to challenge the ideological construction of femininity and masculinity and cling to a romantic conception of heterosexual love as the basis of a new, 'socialist' family.

Historically, as Maxine Molyneux has argued, the more radical (if utopian) elements of Marx and Engels's views have been forgotten in official thinking about the family in those societies that have tried to implement a socialist programme for women's emancipation.[14] Socialist societies have endorsed policies based on what she terms a rigid codification of only the more conservative elements drawn from Engels and Lenin and have left untouched the problems of the sexual division of labour and definitions of sexuality and parenthood.

Socialists in Britain, as in other Western capitalist countries, have found it impossible to maintain a purely critical stance on the family. In the nineteenth and twentieth centuries the labour movement has consistently struggled to protect this most popular of working-class institutions, when necessary at the expense of the interests of women workers. Any call to 'smash the family' is usually perceived not only as romantic anarchism but as vanguardist and patronizing in its rejection of a choice so clearly made by the working class. Criticism of this choice is said to smack of the unsavoury rhetoric of 'false consciousness'. In the *Realpolitik* of contemporary class struggle we cannot afford the luxury of an uncompromising attack on the family.

In so far as contemporary socialists in Britain are adopting a more critical stance now, it is largely through the influence of feminism. The women's liberation movement has drawn attention to the violence and degradation hidden within the walls of the nuclear household, and to the broader social and economic inequalities connected with it. These arguments belong to a long tradition in feminist thought and reflect a long-standing concern with the sexual objectification of women and the exploitation of wives and mothers.

However, the history of feminism presents us with many contradictions on these questions. Many feminists, as Margaret Walters suggests in the cases of Wollstonecraft, Martineau and de Beauvoir,[15] have found it difficult to reconcile their knowledge that femininity was socially constructed with the contradictory situations in which they as women found

---

[14] 'Socialist Societies Old and New: Progress Towards Women's Emancipation', *Feminist Review*, no. 8, summer 1981.

[15] 'The Rights and Wrongs of Women: Mary Wollstonecraft, Harriet Martineau, Simone de Beauvoir', in J. Mitchell & Oakley, eds., *The Rights and Wrongs of Women*, Harmondsworth 1976.

themselves. This subjective tension is reproduced in the conflict, endemic in the history of feminism, between two different approaches to strategy. Should feminists, recognizing that women and men occupy 'separate spheres' of social life, press for proper appreciation of women's work and responsibilities in the family, and for the revaluing of non-aggressive 'feminine' principles? Or should they reject this artificial, socially constructed separation and press for equality *tout court* rather than for equality in difference? These two views dominate the history, as well as the current debates, of feminist thought and practice. They are of central importance for understanding the vexed place of the family in feminism. Many feminists identify the family as a primary site, if not *the* primary site, of women's oppression and seek to abolish it (no doubt the 'world campaign' referred to earlier). Many others argue that feminism must recognize that the majority of women are not helplessly trapped in the family but have willingly identified marriage, children and a family with their own happiness, and it is to this reality that feminism must be made relevant.

A further problem for any feminism set on an uncompromising challenge to the family is that women are divided by the different types of family form characteristic of specific class, ethnic and generational groups. What right does a white feminist have to criticize the family conventions of the Asian community in Britain? What right does a bourgeois woman have to challenge trade-union policies on a 'family wage' that many working-class women support? Is it divisive for young feminists to write off a family form that their mothers had far less choice about? These problems are serious ones, and their consequence is that feminists, however critical we may be of existing structures and ideologies of the family, can reach no consensus on strategic demands, policies or action. Hence with feminism, as with socialism, there is no united call for the abolition of the family – and those who represent this demand as universally supported by either feminists or socialists are addressing themselves to an imaginary consensus.

2. The Appeal of the Family

The lesson we can learn from the ambivalence of socialism and feminism towards the family is that we cannot overestimate the popularity of the family. Familism is not a ruling-class or patriarchal ideology repressively foisted on an unwilling population. Or, if we do consider familism an ideology, we need a theory of ideology that casts people as participants rather than as passive consumers. The Frankfurt School drew attention to the dangers of assuming that ideology is a synonym for illusion: 'Like every proper ideology, the family too was more than a mere lie.'[16]

We do not see the family as an artificial solution to 'false needs', be these theorized in terms of consumerism or state control or whatever. We see investment in the family as an easily comprehended, indeed highly rational, choice, given the material and ideological privilege accorded to it in our society. Although we would want to argue that many – not necessarily all – of the needs currently met in families are historically constructed, they are none the less valid.

Let us envisage the family, then, as 'more than a mere lie'. We shall see the many arguments that can be made, and often enough have been made, against this institution. In what does its appeal consist? Any attempt to think through this question must necessarily be vulnerable to the charges of subjectivism and of generalizing from specific impressions, but we think the risk is worth taking.

Emotional Security

In the first place, it seems to us, the family offers a range of emotional and experiential satisfactions not available elsewhere in the present organization of social relations. The ties of kinship are ascriptive and offer us no choice in the selection of the individuals to whom we relate in this way. Although this may be experienced, no doubt, as constraining, it also – by

---

[16] 'The Family', in *Aspects of Sociology*, London 1973, p. 138.

definition – offers a security not found in other relationships. In the well-known words of Ogden Nash: 'Home is where when you have to go there they have to take you in'. Kinship relations, however weakened in the contemporary 'nuclear' family, still operate at this level. You may easily ignore relatives that you don't like, but they cannot be disposed of completely.

This lack of choice, while prey to many difficulties, provides a level of security often found nowhere else. Relations between kin retain elements of rights and obligations not present elsewhere. It is often recognized that parents, and particularly mothers, are emotionally dependent upon their children. Yet the dependence of children, adult children, upon their parents is much less widely recognized. The acute unease of adult children on the break-up of a family home they have long since left, the grief resulting from a parent's death, are signs of a dependence – an assumption of security – little expressed and regarded as somewhat unfashionable. It is almost as if children may choose to reject the parental home but the parents are expected to continue to provide it as a minimal security for the adult child. The taken-for-grantedness of this security constitutes one aspect of the appeal of the family in a more general sense.

Related to this there is, quite simply, the pleasure of the familiar. It can be known in advance that the individual characteristics of family members will be displayed in a predictable fashion, apparently to the mutual reassurance of all concerned. A will drink too much, B will weep, C is sure to say something tactless, D will be charming and smooth things over. The properties of these people are familiar to us. All the more delight, then, when a second order of familiarity can be identified – when these individually characteristic forms of behaviour can be attributed to the known effects of the parents, or a continuity of family history evoked. An obvious feature of this is the interest in family likeness so regularly evinced. What does it mean, this desire to remark that a child has its father's eyes, mother's hands or some mannerism from a long-dead uncle? Genetic inheritance is clearly fascinating enough, but this represents something more. It is not a search for the inbred likeness of a dynastic inheritance (the notorious Hapsburg chin, for instance); it is a desire for outward tokens of similarity, familiarity and belonging.

The family also provides, in the particular meaning attached to the institution of marriage, an opportunity for the expression of emotional need not legitimate elsewhere. A degree of dependency and vulnerability, for men as well as women, is seen as natural and proper to the shared intimacy and joint investment of marriage. The expression of childlike needs and the exposure of adult weaknesses is held to cement the bond of interdependency characteristic of long-lived marriage. Those whose marriage ends, with death or separation, justifiably feel most acutely the absence not only of physical support and intimacy, but of the sharing of trivial daily anxieties and experiences. The considerable social pressure not to express such needs in other ways – to maintain in all social situations the demeanour of competence and self-sufficiency – adds particularly to the strength of marriage as a means for meeting these evident emotional needs.

It is obviously impossible to say whether, in evoking the supportive intimacy of marriage, we refer to an ideology or the lived experience. Some marriages are exploitative and destructive, others supportive and rewarding. Far from decrying the latter, we see the opportunity for warmth and interdependency as a major factor in the appeal of marriage and family life. The concentration of all such needs into marriage certainly has disadvantages: it leads to very high expectations of marriage, frequently disappointed, and it lessens and delegitimates the emotional value of relationships outside a narrowly defined heterosexual pair-bond. Yet in a social situation where marriage has this privileged meaning, it is by no means surprising that so much is invested in it.

Children

A second major aspect of the appeal of the family must surely lie in its claim to be the most supportive and rewarding means of having and raising children. This works at several different levels. At the most material level it is clearly the case that a married couple can provide a quality of life for their children far higher than that available to most single parents. For the moment we take as given (although it is a very significant 'given') the present social system, which consistently privileges a male breadwinner and a financially dependent wife who takes the primary responsibility for child-care. These duties and privileges are built into the division of labour in employment and into provision for state support. They create a situation where the standard of living in general, and the quality of child-care, will undoubtedly be higher for those raising children in a nuclear family than for those attempting to do so as single employed parents or as dependants of the state.

To this obvious financial advantage must be added the accumulated strength of feeling that children 'need two parents'. The social, ideological and cultural weight attached to this is immense. Children lacking two parents *in situ* in the family home are an object of pity and a source of anxiety. As well as being materially deprived, children will lack stability, a guiding presence and a source of weekend treats. Those who are motherless will obviously not be looked after properly. But the real worry underlying the situation is the obscurely felt conviction that children will not grow up satisfactorily without the presence of a same-sex parent with whom to identify. Hence girls without mothers, and boys without fathers, are the greatest worry of all. (How will these children acquire the 'facts of life' properly, without a gruff fatherly chat about wet dreams or an informed motherly introduction to period pains?)

The strength of these convictions can be seen in the efforts made to remedy the lack when it arises. The decreasing stigma attached to illegitimacy, the tendency for custody to be awarded to the mother in a situation of increasing marital breakdown, and the higher expectation of independence for women, all combine to produce the problem of fatherless families as the most common one. By and large the problem of the 'single-parent family' is one of a woman raising children on her own. One locality in London maintains a scheme to help with these families: entitled, rather unctuously, the 'Big Friend, Little Friend' project, it sends nice men out after school and at weekends to form a relationship with fatherless children and to play the role of a surrogate father or uncle. The practices of agencies concerned with the placing of children uniformly reflect these ideas. Adoption societies, now in a position to be extremely choosy in their selection of parents, tend to regard it as scandalous even to consider as parents people other than a youngish married couple. While custody awards will as a rule be made to the mother, especially of very young children, a father who remarries and can offer the children a normal family home may well prevail over the claims of the original mother. One of the organizations seeking to reverse what they see as an ominous row of victories for women in respect of matrimonial property and custody rights has chosen a name – Families Need Fathers – that seeks to capitalize on this to further its own sectional interests.

The desirability of a child-rearing system based on the presence of two parents (natural or surrogate) has come to supersede the desirability of children being raised by their own kin. In the event of illegitimacy, orphaning or desertion it was common in the nineteenth century for a child to be brought up by other family members – assimilated to a family of cousins or raised by grandparents or even a single aunt or uncle. Although in the nineteenth century novel these children are often depicted as exploited and unappreciated, there can be no doubt that the system itself was normatively sanctioned, for they invariably turn out to be paragons of social and moral worth. In *Dombey and Son*, old Solomon Gills is by today's measure a very bizarre and inadequate parenting resource but Walter nevertheless turns out to be an excellent and upstanding fellow. Fanny Price endures many deprivations at the hands of her superior relatives, the Bertrams, in *Mansfield Park*, but emerges as the emblem of true virtue and morality. Now, however, an ideologically correct representation of parent-hood and the family is seen as far more important for successful child-rearing than biological ties of kinship. In this sense, as far as child-rearing is concerned, we now attach less weight to families themselves but much more to an ideology of familialism.[17]

It is difficult not to relate this shift to the broad social diffusion, and misrepresentation, of psychoanalytic theory. Above all, it seems, we now fear that a child brought up without a mother- and a father-figure will be incapable of identification and will not learn its gender identity properly or even develop a fully mature personality. This is sometimes thought to be based on the Freudian theory that personality development involves the resolution of the Oedipus complex, transcending the conflicting relations with the two parents by an identification with the parent of the same sex. So individual role-models are thought to be necessary for the socialization of the child, and where they are missing, surrogates are searched out. But this is an extremely literal reading of Freud, and a rather implausible one. (We shall come back in chapter 3 to more general questions about psychoanalysis and the family.)

The Appeal of the Natural

The third level at which investment in the family is extremely important is related to affectivity and procreation, but is somewhat more abstract than these as we have described them. It is simply this: that at one and the same time the family is seen as naturally given and as socially and morally desirable. The realms of the 'natural' and the socio-moral are nowhere so constantly merged and confused as in our feelings and thoughts about the family. On many other questions the two would be rigidly separated. Hunger, disease, cruelty and killing appear with great regularity in the natural world but it is seen as distinctively human – a mark of the progress of civilization – to try to eradicate them. With the family it is quite the reverse, for the moral and hence socio-political claims of the family rest

[17] Throughout this book we make a distinction between *familism* and *familization* on the one hand and *familialism* and *familialization* on the other. The former refer to the propagation of politically pro-family ideas and the strengthening of families themselves. The latter refer to ideologies modelled on what are thought to be family values and the rendering of other social phenomena like families.

in large part precisely on its being seen as a biological unit rather than a social arrangement. Considerable social effort is put into defining the boundaries of the 'natural' and in decrying things that fall outside them – be it incest, celibacy or homosexuality – as unnatural. The conventions of romantic love are drenched in appeals to the 'natural' properties of moonlight and nightingales – appeals often stretching the limits of credibility, as when Buddy Holly (taking some artistic licence with natural history) blithely argues: 'Don't you know that the birds and the bees/Go by twos through life's mysteries/So think it over . . .'!

It is in the realm of gender, sexuality, marriage and the family that we are collectively most seduced by appeals to the natural. In this realm the shifting mores of practice are solidified, some to be sanctified and others condemned. The prevailing form of family is seen as inevitable, as naturally given and biologically determined. As such, however, it is imbued with a unique social and moral force, since it is seen as the embodiment of general human values rather than the conventions of a particular society. The image of the family in contemporary society relies heavily on this combination of the natural and the moral. The characteristics of motherhood are particularly heavily invested with connotations of maternal instinct, of self-sacrifice to the propagation of the species, of values superior to mundane self-interest.

Many sociological accounts of the family evoke this aura of a little world immune from the vulgar cash-nexus of modern society, and indeed the family is frequently described as a repository of pre-capitalist values. Ferdinand Tönnies, who first formulated the distinction between 'community' and 'society' that was to be so influential in sociology, waxed lyrical on the natural (but at the same time spiritually elevated) qualities of the mother.[18] Christopher Lasch conjures up an important dimension of this natural/moral relation in his romantic evocation of transcendence: 'Whereas in earlier times the family passed along the dominant values but unavoidably

---

[18] F. Tönnes, *Community and Society*, New York 1963 (first published 1887).

provided the child with a glimpse of a world that transcended them, crystallized in the rich imagery of maternal love, capitalism in its late stages has eliminated or at least softened this contradiction'.[19] The moral qualities of the traditional family are briefly encapsulated in the account given by the Frankfurt School when they write: 'Under the pressure of the father children were supposed to learn not to conceive failures in terms of their societal causation, but to stop at the individual aspect and to render this absolute in terms of guilt, inadequacy, and personal inferiority. If this pressure was not too harsh, and above all, if it was softened by maternal tenderness, then this resulted in human beings who were also capable of seeing faults in themselves; human beings who learned through the father's example an attitude of independence, a joy in free dispositions and inner discipline; who could represent authority as well as freedom and could practise these. Where the family was adequate to its tasks, they gained a conscience, a capacity to love, and consistency. This was productive and progressive'.[20]

It is no coincidence that this mid-nineteenth-century form of the family – the ideal-type against which sociologists measure the operations of other family forms – is the same as the paradigmatic family of contemporary ideology. This family of desire and myth is not the brutal rule of a patriarch over an extended household, nor is it an aggregation of faceless and ineffective individuals. It has an orderly division of labour between husband and wife, and a firm but kindly style with the children that will be good for them in the long run. It is today's equivalent of the nineteenth-century bourgeois ideal. It appears in child-care manuals, in advertisements for cars and insurance policies, in the formal and the 'hidden' curricula of schools, in the catalogues of Mothercare and the brochures of travel agents. This is not to say that it is not genuinely desired or that those who desire it are brainwashed by ideology. On the

---

[19] *Haven in a Heartless World*, New York 1977, p. xvii.
[20] 'The Family', p. 141. This very interesting essay provides in summary form a preview of Lasch's main argument and has the additional advantage of giving due recognition to the exploitativeness and brutality – to women and children – of this form of family.

contrary. Few people wish their children to be deviants, misfits, delinquents or suicides. In our society this model of family, however successfully it may actually be realized, offers the most plausible system for rearing children who will be competent and secure, stable and self-sufficient. In this context such a family will inevitably be more than a myth, a dream, a hope – the myth is instructive, the dream pleasurable and the hope rational.

3. A Familialized Society

The image of the family as a broken-down carthorse – merely a quaint reminder of an earlier era – conjured up by those who bemoan its crisis and decline, is entirely misleading. As we shall show in the next chapter, the family remains a vigorous agency of class placement and an efficient mechanism for the creation and transmission of gender inequality. In addition to this, and perhaps even more importantly for an understanding of the contemporary family, this institution is the focal point of a set of ideologies that resonate throughout society. The imagery of idealized family life permeates the fabric of social existence and provides a highly significant, dominant and unifying, complex of social meaning.

At the most general level this can be seen in the correspondences between the division of labour in the home and that found in paid employment. Many feminists have remarked that the work that women do for wages is, by and large, nothing other than domestic labour in a different context. Where there is cooking, cleaning, nursing the sick, minding and teaching small children, sewing, servicing men and being charming to be done – there will women be found. The pattern can be easily observed in any institution such as a hospital or school. The structure of job-segregation corresponds closely to the pattern of the domestic division of labour. So secretaries spend much of their time making life easier for their bosses: preparing and clearing up work, reminding of appointments, smoothing over the atmosphere in the office. Nurses deal with dirt, disease, people's bodies and their troubles, while doctors inspect the records and make the decisions. The jobs that the women do call for deference, taking orders, fitting in with a man's requirements. The same sort of story could be told in almost every public sphere. The dramatic victory of the Socialist Party in the French presidential and legislative elections of 1981, for instance, has resulted in a government with more women in positions of considerable power. They are to be found in the ministries of the family, of women's rights, and of consumption.

Twentieth-century children who have the misfortune to be brought up in residential institutions rather than in their own homes are raised in a curious simulation of family life. Gone are the mass regimes, the hideous marshalling of great collectivities described so clearly in accounts of similar institutions in the nineteenth century. The young Jane Eyre's first impressions of Lowood School convey this sense of large numbers most strikingly: 'We came upon the hum of many voices, and presently entered a wide, long room, with great deal tables, two at each end, on each of which burnt a pair of candles, and seated all round on benches, a congregation of girls of every age, from nine or ten, to twenty. Seen by the dim light of the dips, their number to me appeared countless, though not in reality exceeding eighty'.[21] The ten-year-old child of today, entering any institution from a local authority children's home to a public school, will more likely be confronted by an organization split into self-consciously 'family units' complete with house-parents and pseudo-siblings. Enlightened opinion insists that a re-creation, or emulation, of the ethos of family life is necessary for such an upbringing.

It is noteworthy, too, that the organization of authority in non-residential schools is now often closely based on a model of the family rather than, as is sometimes thought, operating in strong contrast to it. Frequently a distinction is made between the executive and disciplinary powers of the headmaster and

[21] Charlotte Brontë, *Jane Eyre*, Harmondsworth 1966, p. 76.

the pastoral and mediating duties of a senior mistress. Appointment procedures for these senior posts recognize explicitly the desirability of this patently parental division of authority and care, and it has increasingly become the norm in co-educational schools (themselves, of course, increasingly replacing single-sex schools).

Examples such as these serve to demonstrate the point that the structure and values of family life play a very important part in the organization and ethos of institutions rightly thought of as 'social' but wrongly contrasted with the family as an exclusively 'private' affair. No such opposition between family and society exists. Just as the family has been socially constructed, so society has been familialized. Indeed it can be argued that in contemporary capitalist society one dominant set of social meanings is precisely an ideology of familialism. The meaning of family life extends far beyond the walls of concrete households in which the proverbial 'co-residing close kin' go about their business of marrying and raising children.

It is hardly necessary to point to the saturation of the media, advertising and popular entertainment in familial ideology. Situation comedies based on single girls or bachelor flats operate on the assumption that Mr and Mrs Average, watching these bizarre individuals from the security of their familial sitting-room, will find it *intrinsically* funny that a man should be staggering down to the launderette or a woman attempting to change a light bulb. Many of the most popular series on television and radio are essentially dramatizations of family life in which a delicate balance of stability and change is carefully secured. The level of sophistication may vary from *Crossroads* to *Soap* but the recuperation of family values is common to both – as it is to the advertisements by which such programmes are framed and interrupted. Advertising has been subjected to several critical studies, with regard to the construction of gender.[22] All too well known is the banal and

[22] Trevor Millum. *Images of Women*. London 1975; Erving Goffman, *Gender Advertisements*, London 1979; Judith Williamson, *Decoding Advertisements*, London 1978.

repetitious theme of the perfect family found in conventional advertisements for soap powder and breakfast cereals. Time after time, images of the satisfactions of conjugality and parenthood are created and re-created in the mode of the moment.

The popularity of familialism can hardly be doubted. The monarchy, for instance, is held to be a very popular institution in contemporary Britain and the emotion surrounding it is certainly pandered to (some would say orchestrated by) the media. Yet it is not the monarchy as such that is popular – the British public has no particular obsession with divine rulers, royal blood or solitary crowned heads. It is not the institution of monarchy that is popular, it is the royal family. The monarchy was severely threatened when Edward VIII abdicated in the face of the opposition to his taking a divorcee as queen, and it has taken decades of indefatigable royal family life to secure the present popularity of the institution. The members of the royal family move in a world that is a fairy-tale yet familiar. The need to break down the barriers between glamorous fiction and daily life as it is lived in ordinary households is constantly catered for in this ceaseless interplay of fiction and reality. Idealized, yet flawed, perfection with personal foibles, these characters represent a way of managing the contradiction between family life as we are told it should be and family life as all too often experienced.

It will not do to put forward a conspiracy theory of the media. It is clearly the case that the familial ideology expressed in the rigid stereotypes of unreformed children's reading schemes, or in popular romantic fiction, is barely recognizable as having anything to do with the families most people live in. In the ideal world of Janet and John we may now find Daddy helping with the dishes but we will not find Mummy where she empirically is – out at work. If there were a direct correspondence between the imagery of the family represented in the media and the actual composition of households, we would find the majority of the population living in nuclear residences of children and their parents. Yet, if the 1971 census is to be believed, fewer than a third of Britain's households were enmeshed in such an arrangement and only one in ten was organized in the normatively sanctioned pattern of paternal breadwinner and maternal full-time housewife. We live in a society where the 'average family' is continually evoked. We are continually addressed as belonging to it, by the left and the labour movement as much as from any other source. Take the case of the recent disarmament poster that announces: 'The average British family spent £16 a week last year on arms'. Predictably it is illustrated by an image of a typical family whose supermarket trolley contains a miniature missile nestling among the groceries. Why are we addressed in this way rather than as individual tax-payers with no control over the proportion of our taxes allocated to defence? Because 'the family' is a so much more resonant image. The poster tries to construct an association between domesticity, family values and pacifism. We are to be shocked at this militaristic invasion of the sanctity of hearth and home. And indeed we are. But to couch the message in the discourse of familialism is to mask the fact that single people will also die in a nuclear war and that it is as citizens and not as families that we should be protesting about arms spending.

It should be remembered that the currently dominant model of the family is not timeless and culture-free. This model reflects a form of family characteristic of the nineteenth-century bourgeoisie. Mark Poster has referred to it as one of four forms of family extant in western Europe since the middle ages and has stressed the way in which this particular form has spread across social classes.[23] This hegemonic family form is a powerful ideological force that mirrors in an idealized way the characteristics attributed to contemporary family life. It has only a tenuous relation to co-residence and the organization of

---

[23] *Critical Theory of the Family*, London 1978. In fact the hegemonizing 'spread' of the model can still be seen in the fascinating spectacle of the current ideological *embourgeoisement* of the royal family. Buckingham Palace, bearer of the traditional aristocratic disdain for an exclusive child-mother bond and accustomed to assign the care of royal children to servants, has discovered that the Princess of Wales will not go on the lengthy foreign tour planned for 1983 unless she is allowed to take her baby with her.

34

households as economic units. It dominates, rather than is dominated by, the social organization of kinship. The major significance of 'the family' in Britain today is ideological. Kate Ellis puts this point very clearly in her critical response to the pro-family lobby on the American left: 'The question is: is there anything we *all* want from the family, be we married or single, straight or gay, male or female, "good" or "bad", right or left? I would answer: only in so far as "the family" is perceived not as any particular (and thus mutable) living arrangement, but as the institution that can cure all our social and personal ills, a metaphor for some private and public paradise lost.'[24] The mythological character of 'the family' is part and parcel of its ideological dominance. The appeal to cultural universality and a biologically grounded timelessness is extremely strained. As Jane Collier, Michelle Rosaldo and Sylvia Yanagisako have pointed out, the ideological construction of the family as the antithesis to the cash-nexus could *only* refer to a capitalist society.[25]

4. Confronting Nature?

What constraints apply to any fundamental reorganization of the family or to the goal of abolishing it? To what extent do the biology of human reproduction or the psychic patterns of human maturation constitute a procrustean bed on which all social arrangements must ultimately rest?

The category of 'the natural' plays a part in many con- temporary institutions and is used in many social situations: the concept of 'natural justice' in law; the educational philo- sophy of the 'natural unfolding' of the child; even the pursuit of

---

[24] 'Can the Left Defend . . .?', p. 17.
[25] 'We can hardly be speaking of a universal notion of The Family shared by people everywhere and for all time because people everywhere and for all time have not participated in market relations out of which they have constructed a contrastive notion of the family.' ('Is There a Family? New Anthropological Views', Barrie Thorne and Marilyn Yalom, eds., *Rethinking the Family: Some Feminist Questions*, New York 1982, p. 35.)

'natural childbirth'. But nowhere is this category so constantly invoked, and invoked precisely to sanction and strengthen the existing social arrangement, as in the case of the family. Nowhere else is the natural met with such passivity, complacency and moral approbation. In few other areas is it extolled as superior to the creations of humanity.

Leaving aside for a moment the question of whether social agency is normally, or should be, passive in the face of nature, we need to question the meaning of 'natural' as a description of the family. The Frankfurt School correctly pointed out that the family is quintessentially a social rather than a natural unit, and they added that the tendency to hypostatize the family as natural goes back to the Enlightenment: 'At first sight the family appears in history as a relationship of natural origin, which then differentiates itself to become modern monogamy and which by virtue of this differentiation founds a special domain, the domain of private life. For naive consciousness this private life appears as an island in the midst of the social dynamics, a residue of the state of nature, as it has been idealized. In reality the family not only depends on the historically concrete social reality, but is socially mediated down to its innermost structure.'[26] To designate the family as natural is as irrelevant as to designate it as pre-capitalist. The family is no more 'biological' than the recently developed soap powder proudly claiming this attribute. One almost feels that nature is invoked simply because the family is so closely allied to the undeniably natural process of biological reproduction. Yet eating is just as undeniably natural and no one would think of assigning restaurants or groceries to this category. Appeals to nature are commonly made in resistance to social change. (The invention of the steam-engine was greeted in some quarters with the fear that the human frame would physically disintegrate if propelled with such unnatural velocity.) We may legitimately be suspicious of them. 'Nature', observed Virginia Woolf cynically, 'is now known to vary greatly in her commands and to be largely under control.'[27] Certainly, as far

---

[26] 'The Family', p. 130.
[27] *Three Guineas*, London 1978. p. 203.

as the familiy is concerned, the commands of nature revealed in anthropology, history and zoology are extremely varied and contradictory.

The crux of the argument from biology is the notion that the division of labour between women and men in the process of procreation must necessarily lead to long periods in which women are dependent on men for protection and support. Without denying the physical and mental demands of pregnancy, childbirth, lactation and child-care, we can properly question the assumption that these inevitably lead to women's dependence. In a society where contraception was readily available, where medical technology was geared towards minimizing the rigours of childbirth, where the breast-feeding of infants in public was not regarded as a social solecism, and where children were cared for equally by men and women – and where responsibility for children was not used systematically to block women's employment prospects – the material conditions of women's dependence on men would not exist. The fact that we do not live in such a society is not to be laid at the door of biology: it is a *political* question.

Sebastiano Timpanaro, justifiably irritated by the idealism permeating twentieth-century Marxism, has recently argued that we need to take greater account of the determination over human action of the physical and biological world.[28] He counters the optimistic strain in Marxism – the assertion that human labour transcends nature – with a gloomy reminder of famine, disease, death and the cruelties and sufferings inflicted by nature on even the most civilized societies. His intervention is a thought-provoking one for feminists. Does his argument imply that feminists, too, suffer from idealistic illusions when they assert the possibility that reproductive biology need not have the social consequences it has had in the past? Or does it imply that these questions fall within the field of contemporary scientific application – a field in which we should be engaged in a more informed and committed way? Timpanaro's argument, although a salutary one, remains couched at a frustratingly

[28] *On Materialism*, London, 1975.

abstract level, and we would agree with Kate Soper's insistence on the social mediation of these natural phenomena. 'Even death', she writes, 'that notorious leveller, will not lay down in the flatness of its essence.'[29] Certainly maternal and infant mortality is not a stark and simple fact of nature, but is susceptible to social control and historical variation. Famine may be a natural given of the pre-social world but we know nonetheless that a more just distribution of the world's food resources could eradicate it. The diseases of the undernourished are every bit as social as the nervous breakdowns and heart diseases of the affluent.

It is not simply that the facts of nature are amenable to at least a substantial degree of social control. Appeals to nature, and particularly to natural inequality, have a hallowed tradition in the justification and legitimation of social inequality and social division. This has been widely recognized in the history of ideologies of class, estate, race and nationality. The irreducible differences between the sexes provide a fertile basis for such legitimating processes: 'The pattern of gender relations in our society is overwhelmingly a social rather than a natural one, but it is a social construction that caricatures biological difference in the most grotesque way and then appeals to this misrepresented natural world for its own justification.'[30]

Nowhere can this process of caricature and misrepresentation be seen more clearly than in the recently fashionable science of socio-biology. In categorizing the family as 'anti-social', and in accusing it (somewhat anthropomorphically no doubt) of being a 'selfish' institution, we invite the socio-biological retort that selfish mechanisms are inevitably the means by which 'selfish genes' seek to reproduce themselves. Socio-biology seeks to demonstrate that all human behaviour is explicable in terms of the tendency of genes – DNA – to

[29] 'Marxism, Materialism and Biology', in John Mepham and David Hillel Ruben, eds., *Issues in Marxist Philosophy*, vol. 2, Brighton 1979, p. 95
[30] Michèle Barrett, *Women's Oppression Today*, London 1980, p. 76.

38

maximize the conditions of survival and reproduction.[31] Sex difference is written into socio-biology at a fundamental level. Males, who are capable of fathering countless children, will naturally be sexually promiscuous in order to populate the world with their genetic successors; at the same time they will guard against the social obligations of fatherhood unless they can be sure the child is theirs. Females, whose reproductive capacities are finite, will seek to maximize them by selecting a reliable and well-providing mate and will not threaten the genetic succession by sexual deviation. To this elemental model we find accommodated explanations of the minute details of contemporary sexual and familial behaviour. As Lucy Bland points out, the theory enables socio-biologists to justify as natural the various trappings of present definitions of femininity and masculinity. Female coyness, male philandering, criteria of female attractiveness and so on – down to the finest details of male fantasy – are scientifically explained in articles in *Playboy* as well as in more scholarly publications.[32] Socio-biology is shot through with a political conservatism that waxes lyrical on the stupidity and ignorance of feminism, which it sees as attempting to halt (like Canute the tides) the necessary passage of genetic evolution. As is the case with a considerable body of work in palaeontology, primatology, evolutionary anthropology and so on, the 'findings' of socio-biology bear a suspiciously close resemblance to the sexist principles and assumptions of its practitioners.

Feminists have paid considerable attention to the sexist bias of natural, particularly biological, science in both its erudite and popular forms and it is not necessary for us to take up these arguments one by one. It must be repeated, however, that the argument from biology can be countered on a different level – that of social and political choice. It is a mark of progress that issues such as eugenics, abortion, euthanasia, the artificial preservation of life and the treatment of severely disabled

[31] Richard Dawkins, *The Selfish Gene*, London 1976; E.O. Wilson, *On Human Nature*, New York, 1978.

[32] ''It's Only Human Nature''? Socio-biology and Sex Differences', *Schooling and Culture*, no.10, summer 1981.

babies are now recognized as not simply scientific or medical problems, but as matters of political and moral debate. A central concern of feminism must surely be to ensure that questions to do with sexuality and procreation are wrested from the grip of biology and defined as political matters. Underlying a conception of the family as a natural or biological unit is a much broader tendency to think of the family in essentialist terms. It is as if we recognize variation in family forms as only the surface appearance of something that, in essence, is common to all human society. We assume the family to be something we *discover* in all societies – immutably there. Yet it is unclear what the essence of 'the family' would be if we tried to define it as a universal. The variation of kinship arrangements documented by anthropologists renders even the loosest definition impossible. Certainly it would be fallacious to assume that 'the family' inevitably follows the pattern of the small-scale domestic household characteristic of contemporary Britain, and even more insular to imagine that notions of breadwinning men and dependent wives are historical universals.

The concept of 'the family' is, of course, a fairly recent one and is projected onto other societies replete with anachronisms. Jean-Louis Flandrin has described how, even as short a time ago as the late eighteenth century, the notion of family referring to co-residing close kin simply did not exist. The aristocracy had its lineages and houses and the labouring classes had their ramshackle living arrangements, but only the emergent bourgeoisie had an orderly domestic life and the generational transmission of occupational status characteristic of the modern meaning of 'the family'.[33] To talk of 'the pre-capitalist family' let alone 'the eskimo family' or 'the nomadic family' is to impose an essential similarity on highly diverse institutions and practices.[34]

It is a sign of the power of essentialist – and highly

[33] *Families in Former Times*, London 1979.
[34] Rayna Rapp, Ellen Ross and Renate Bridenthal, 'Examining Family History', *Feminist Studies*, vol. 5, no.1, 1979.

naturalistic – views of the family that many writers on the subject (including ourselves) find it difficult to avoid essentialist formulations even when consciously attempting to do so. This is merely another indication of the strength and tenacity of the ideology of familialism in our culture. We are not like those early explorers of Africa who could no more identify the sexual mores of the native peoples with their own family experience than they could recognize the religious behaviour they found as comparable to their own Christianity. We, it seems, are ever prone to construct other societies and earlier epochs of our own in the images of a familialism from which we cannot escape.

5. Family Values and the Left

The left, of course, is not immune from any of these elements of the appeal of the family. Like society in general, the contemporary left is familialized, and sections of it are familist. Socialists and feminists have borrowed the terminology of family relationships, not to stress – as the church tends to do – authority relations between the generations but to emphasize solidarity. Sisterhood and brotherhood, and the forms of address these concepts give rise to, are important metaphors in the majority of anti-capitalist and radical movements. They represent positive aspirations towards a unity that must overcome any personal dislikes or differences. They indicate relationships not contracted on a mercenary basis but founded on the necessity of learning to live and work with, if not to love, others who share a common cause. Many socialist utopias invoke positive images of the family as a metaphor for a genuinely communitarian society. Marx's 'from each according to his ability, to each according to his needs' is an ideal to which the nearest approximation we can imagine is a caring family where the contribution of each is not subjected to exact calculation.

Socialism and feminism are both political movements that depend upon not only a critical analysis of contemporary society but a commitment to a more just, equal and satisfying society. At some level, socialists and feminists assume a relatively optimistic view of human nature in that we believe in the possibility of a more altruistic and caring set of social relations than we see in the world today. There is, we could say, an irreducible politico-moral element – an evaluative dimension – at the heart of the socialist project. It is not difficult to see why the family, representing at its best an ideal of responsibility and affection for others, is seen as the most appropriate metaphor with which to render anti-capitalist values. Given the claims of the family to be the primary site of the priority of feeling over calculation, of altruism rather than selfishness, it would be surprising if things were otherwise.

It is this that leads the most intransigent critics of the present family form to hold out as an inspiration the positive ideal of family values. It is this that leads to continuing ambivalence about the family among socialists and feminists. One way of expressing this is to contrast the 'promise' of the family with the common 'reality', as do Wini Breines, Margaret Cerullo and Judith Stacey when they say: 'Many came to identify feminism with anti-motherhood and anti-family. Yet our most important criticism of the content of contemporary motherhood and family life (the two are inextricable) was that under the present social order they fail to realize their promise. The gap between the promise and the reality of family life was the object of our criticism, a gap we sought to reduce with our experiments with alternative family forms. By exposing this gap, our criticism of the modern family became immediately an attack on a society that makes family ideals impossible to realize. The best of these ideals – intimacy, commitment, nurturance, collectivity, and individual autonomy – were and remain central among feminist objectives.'[35]

It remains a moot point whether these ideals are 'family ideals' or individual and social ideals that the family has arrogated to itself. Linda Gordon and Allen Hunter make a

---

[35] 'Social Biology, Family Studies and Anti-feminist Backlash', *Feminist Studies*, vol. 4, no.1, 1978.

similar point in different terms when they say: 'We also think that socialists should support the search for the satisfactions that families can sometimes provide: emotional and sexual intimacy, child-rearing by caring people, cooperation and sharing. Some people are now searching for and finding these outside families.'[36] To some extent the difference lies in terminology. It is likely that when Gordon and Hunter refer to 'outside families' they refer to what Breines, Cerullo and Stacey describe as 'alternative family forms'. Yet this is not a mere semantic quibble. It will be important to determine whether the positive ideals and satisfactions that we hope to strengthen spring from the family or – as we shall argue – survive in spite of it.

---

[36] 'The New Right', p. 11.

II
The Anti-social Family

1. Inheritance

Almost all of us are born and reared in a family. Those who are not raised by their parents in a private household are brought up in institutions that seek to imitate family life as faithfully as possible. What could be more classless than this universal experience? What could be less divisive? In reality, far from being a social leveller, forging bonds that cut across the barriers of class and sex, the family creates and recreates the very divisions it is often thought to ameliorate.

The family is a class institution and gives us each our initial class position. Each child begins life in the working class or the property-owning class, in the ranks of the professions, or of small business, of the landed aristocracy or of the lowest group of the insecure and unemployed. Most boys will live out their lives in the same class and even in the same section of it; most girls will marry a man in a situation very similar to their own father's.

The main way in which social classes reproduce themselves over time is by bearing and rearing children. This is why Engels associated the historical origin of the modern monogamous family (in which a women has only one husband) with the origin of private property and class. 'The rule of the man in the family, the procreation of children who could only be his, destined to be the heirs of his wealth – these alone were frankly avowed by the Greeks as the exclusive aims of monogamy'.[1]

[1] 'Origin of the Family, Private Property and the State', in *Marx and Engels: Selected Works*, London 1968, p. 502.

There have sometimes been classes and social groups that were reproduced by recruitment rather than by birth: the celibate clergy of the Catholic world, slaves in the Americas while the capturing of slaves in Africa continued, immigrant workers in many parts of Western Europe where settlement is discouraged. Such classes and groups are exceptionally weak and powerless. Even the Catholic Church was weaker than its vast wealth and tenacious ideological grip would have enabled it to be. Indeed it can be argued that in the heyday of the Church priestly celibacy was enjoined precisely in order to maintain the access of the great secular families to its highest offices and so to retain the church as a whole in a position of client. Slave groups and ethnic minorities that reproduce themselves, though exploited and down-trodden, are at least able to develop some forms of accommodation and adaptation over generations. So inheritance of class position serves to establish and to domesticate class divisions.

Of course people's class position is not fixed by their parentage. Some may move from one class to another, and many move up and down the ladder of status and security within the working class and into the ambiguous positions of bureaucrats, accounts clerks, scientists, managers. In fact the expansion of these last categories during the twentieth century was achieved largely by recruitment from below and required a large amount of upward mobility. The expansion is now slowing down and it seems unlikely that such rates of mobility will be seen again. But the experience of social fluidity, the apparent breaking of old class destinies, personified in the career of the grammar-school boy and the success of the working man's son at a redbrick university, has left its mark in popular consciousness. Education has become seen as the main road to success in life. It is what you do rather than where you are that counts.

What is deceptive about this social imagery is that it is too strongly coloured by the exceptions – those who move – and it ignores what can be taken for granted – that most men follow their fathers. A recent large scale survey[2] found that 62% of the

---

[2] John H. Goldthorpe, *Social Mobility and Class Structure in Modern Britain*, Oxford 1980, pp. 70, 75. The figures relate to sons born between 1938 and 1947.

sons of men who worked as professionals, administrators, managers, supervisors and higher-grade technicians (Class I and II occupations) were in jobs in the same range as their fathers at the time of the study, and only 13% had manual jobs. At the other end of the scale 58% of the sons of men in manual jobs themselves had manual jobs, and only 18% had Class I and II jobs. This was the measure of the extent to which fathers passed on social position to their sons during a period when expansion at the top of the job hierarchy was producing new opportunities. How much more will they do so as those who have made it to the top strive to pass on their advantage to their sons?

It is interesting that families are less effective in passing the father's occupational status on to their daughters. (Unfortunately there is no evidence about how much women follow in their *mother's* footsteps.) Women often marry up or down. 'The typical father from Class I is more likely to see his daugher downwardly mobile than his son, or, to be more precise, to have a son-in-law of lower social class than his son. Conversely, the girl from Classes VI or VIII is more likely to be upwardly mobile than her brother'.[3] And a woman's own occupation is less determined by her father's than is a man's. (The only exception to this is that it is even more difficult for a woman whose father was not a professional or a manager to become one herself than it is for a man.)

Figures like these give a very gross picture of how social classes are reproduced through the family. They do not tell us much about the processes involved. Perhaps the most important process is the way in which families pass on advantage and disadvantage in the chances of educational success.

During the 1950s and 1960s the question of social mobility was a dominant concern among sociologists who studied education. There was socialist concern with equality of opportunity and with showing how the selective system of secondary modern and grammar schools failed in its overt objective of offering such opportunity to pupils from working-class homes. There were some interesting and depressing findings, which in

[3] Anthony Heath, *Social Mobility*, London 1981, p. 113.

the end were interpreted to place the credit or blame for school success on the child's home, and especially on the mother. A working-class family had to have something unusual about it for its children to do well at school. The mother had to be better educated than average, or the parents interested in reading. What is interesting is how these researches showed that parents affected their children's class position even when they did not simply place them in their own. It is a pity there were not more studies of the way in which parents with professional and managerial jobs so often managed to ensure that their children did not fall too far below them – a task which is becoming increasingly difficult as the expansion of these strata slows down. What is depressing is that the researches show even more clearly how family and class are interwoven. The sociologists who were involved in these studies shrank from their full implications. They were reluctant to see that their work constituted an indictment of the family as an institution – the more so since they would have been tempted to read it in moralistic and individualistic terms as an indictment of the working-class families themselves. The next generation of radical sociologists turned its guns towards a more generally acceptable target and developed a critique of the education system and school curricula from a class perspective. (Indeed it is remarkable how the sociology of the family, as a sub-field, fell from favour as left-wing and critical perspectives gained strength within sociology; it is only the advent of the new feminism that has brought it back in.)

Another major process in reproducing classes is the inheritance of wealth. 'It is difficult to avoid the conclusion that inheritance has been the most important single source of wealth inequality in the fairly recent past in twentieth century Britain', according to a study by C.D. Harbury and D.M.W.N. Hitchens.[4] They estimate that 'something between two-thirds and four-fifths of those who died rich in the third quarter of the present century owed their wealth to inheritance, and the rest to entrepreneurship and luck.'[5] Furthermore, daughters who

[4] *Inheritance and Wealth Inequality in Britain*, London 1979, p. 136.
[5] Ibid, p. 131.

inherit wealth frequently marry sons who inherit wealth. So both inheritance between generations and patterns of marriage among inheritors serve to reproduce the concentration of wealth in a small class of people. We have chosen to start at a very general structural level by showing how the family serves to pass on privilege and disadvantage from one generation to the next. We have done this partly because it highlights very clearly how the family embodies the principle of selfishness, exclusion and pursuit of private interest and contravenes those of altruism, community and pursuit of the public good. Society is *divided into* families and the divisions are deep, not merely ones of slight antipathy and mild distrust.

2. Individualism = Familism

Conservative thought is often said to focus on the idea of individualism: self-help, self-support, self-sufficiency, self-respect. It rejects dependence, 'scrounging', collectivism, the belief that 'the world owes you a living'. Yet in practice the unit of self-support is not the individual but the family. In Britain no one nowadays thinks that children, as long as they are being trained or educated, should support themselves. Conservatives think that husbands should support their wives and children and that disabled or old people should be able to turn to their kin for help before they seek help from charity or from the state. Indeed, it has tended to be conservatives who have wished to extend the range of kin among whom mutual aid could be expected and progressives who have made more and more people eligible for public assistance. This is a boundary that has been contested and shifted many times in the last century and a half. At present, officially speaking, only children under sixteen who live with a parent and wives who live with a husband can have no rights to the basic non-insured state social security payments. And still it is conservatives who resist the socialist demand for an adequate child benefit and reject the feminist demand that husband and wife should have independent rights to social security.

Many of the catch-phrases of conservative politics – individual choice in education or in health-care, freedom of choice for consumers, owner-occupation – thus mask a defence of paternal as against social responsibility and authority. For it is not children who choose their education but their parents who 'choose' to give them what education they can afford with the father's income. And so it is with health insurance, with housing and with household consumption. People's standard of living is not determined by their own income but by that of the household they live in and how its income is shared among its members.

In this context children, and to some extent wives, are mere extensions of men. Their needs are defined for them by the head of the family and as part of his needs. A man should not merely be self-supporting but should take care of his dependants as well. He should be expected to be able to earn enough to keep 'a family'. Indeed when a wage is said to be so low that it is below the poverty line what is meant is that it is below the level of social security benefit for a family of two adults and two children, not that the worker himself could not live on it. This idea of the family wage for men is deeply embedded in conservative thought. In part, this is because it helps maintain men's privilege and authority. But it is also because the conflation of the individual and the family is absolutely necessary to sustain the conservative economic fantasy. This is a fantasy of an economy in which the actions of self-seeking 'economic men' add up, through the 'unseen hand' of the market mechanism, to an optimal pattern of production and consumption. In it, each member is motivated by self-interest to contribute to the wants of others. In order to elevate the morality of the market into an entire social ethic, it is necessary to ignore all those members of society who do not themselves enter the market. For most of them this is done by the sleight of hand of subsuming them as members of families into the individuality of their head of household. He can then be assumed to be an economic agent, complete with income, expenditure, consumer preferences, indifference curves and marginal prospensities to all sorts of economic activity. So it becomes possible to believe that the whole economy is organized on the liberal-individualist model of the free market, with everyone working in order to support themselves, because those who cannot earn a living are subsumed under those who can. For socialists, it is dangerous to pretend that society is made up entirely of people who can contribute to production. It masks our interdependence and the necessity of a social conception of needs and a social plan for meeting them. Unfortunately, though, there has been a strong tendency in British socialist thought to accept this form of familism. This is largely due to the fact that socialism has been fostered and shaped in a labour movement dominated by the trade unions of the skilled male workers whose own interests lay in privileging those who *could* (or could claim they could) contribute a great deal to production and who could use the idea of the family wage to claim higher wages for themselves and to exclude women, children and young people from the better paid jobs.[6] The idea of being a 'provider' for the family has also become a cherished element of male working-class self-esteem.

A broader conception of socialism would recognize that this kind of familism merely papers over some of the cracks in the capitalist system, or protects those lucky enough to be in families with a good wage-earner. It does not solve the fundamental problems of the wage system as a means of meeting the needs of the working class: that some people have no wage-earner to depend on, and some wage-earners have no dependants while others have too many. It is a fantasy solution that would work in reality only if each wage-earner had a household of two adults and two-point-four children to support throughout his working life, and the rest of the people were neatly distributed among such households. In other words it would only work if households were formed on some

---

[6] This is discussed more fully in our article 'The Family Wage: Some Problems for Socialists and Feminists', *Capital and Class*, no. 11, 1980.

bureaucratic principle and not, as families, on the basis of kinship.[7]

The confusion of individual and family in conservative thought reflects a close association between the two in everyday life. It is an association that has many pernicious effects. The most marked of these is that children are a private possession. Though they are to join society and be its future members, they are produced by and for their parents. Parents decide how many to have, when to have them and they try to determine how to bring them up. Often they become extensions of their parent's personalities or a compensation for failings in their lives. They can be a major source of pride, or often of disappointment. During childhood this may be rewarding and apparently successful, but as adolescence wears on and the child becomes more independent a unique kind of problem frequently occurs. The resentment that parents feel about the wrong choices their children make is quite unlike any disagreement between other people about how to live or what to do. The sort of behaviour that provokes the cry of despair, 'Why do you treat me like this?', is often not *treating* the parent at all, but simply choosing the wrong life-style, the wrong haircut, the wrong job, the wrong partner. What the children do with their own lives necessarily affects the parents. The biblical notion that when the fathers have eaten a sour grape the children's teeth are set on edge has little resonance today, but its obverse is part of our daily experience.

In this setting of intimate interdependence, it is not surprising that the explanation of individual troubles should be sought in the constellation of the immediate family. Since the 1950s 'family therapy' rather than individual therapy has been the vogue for dealing with difficult or delinquent children and even to some extent with adults who are mentally ill.[8] In many ways this is more appropriate than the individualism of traditional

---

[7] See Mary McIntosh, 'The Welfare State and the Needs of the Dependent Family', in Sandra Burman, ed., *Fit Work for Women*, London 1979. The impossibility of supporting everyone by paying male workers a uniform 'living wage' was first pointed out by Eleanor Rathbone in *The Disinherited Family*, London 1924.

[8] There is a useful discussion of this in Poster, *Critical Theory of the Family*.

therapies, though usually the theory has been that a well-organized family with appropriate parental and gender roles would produce adequate personalities and that any problems could be corrected by bringing the family back into line with the good model. R.D. Laing has used a similar vision of family processes to come to the much more disturbing conclusion that in the close-knit emotional tangle of the nuclear 'family nexus' the confusions of intersubjectivity and the problems of distinguishing oneself from the attributions imposed by those closest to one could result in schizophrenia. In the nuclear family each member 'attempts to regulate the inner life of the other in order to preserve his own'.[9] From Laing's accounts of the families of his schizophrenic patients, it is not hard to see how the tight intimacy of nuclear family life may cause acute problems for family members, even when the solutions they seek are less dramatic than schizophrenia.

Another twist of the screw of familialism and individualism is the way that being reared in an enclosed family, with one parent mainly responsible for the children, tends to produce a highly individualistic personality structure. Critics of more communal forms of childrearing have argued that a close and continuous bond with a single mother-figure during the first few years of life is essential to the development of an adequate personality. John Bowlby described the consequence of maternal deprivation as an 'affectionless personality' incapable of forming intimate one-to-one relationships.[10] René Spitz argued that infants reared in groups became institutionalized and unable to live as individuals without group support.[11] There have been many doubts about this sort of research, which has mostly looked at residential children's institutions on which the inmates are deprived of considerably more than the mother-child bond.[12] But it is often not noticed that even if they were right, the typical personality of the collectively reared

[9] *The Politics of Experience*, London 1967, p. 13.
[10] *Maternal Care and Mental Health*, World Health Organization 1951.
[11] 'Hospitalism: An Inquiry into the Genesis of Psychiatric Conditions in Early Childhood', in *The Psychoanalytic Study of the Child*, New York 1945.
[12] Michael Rutter, ed., *Maternal Deprivation Reassessed*, Harmondsworth 1972.

child might simply be different, not 'inadequate'. Indeed the typical personality of the normal successfully family-reared child may have its undesirable features: a need to form intimate one-to-one ties to the exclusion of a more diffused bond to a wider group, a tendency to go it alone as an individual and a lack of concern for group support and approval or group interests.

Bruno Bettelheim, in *The Children of the Dream*, has provided a balanced study of communal child-rearing in the Israeli kibbutz.[13] He found that the kibbutz-reared generation had more uniform educational attainments, with fewer dramatic successes and fewer 'failures', than other Israelis. 'The personality of the kibbutz-born generation seems depleted. . . [but] these young people seem much less neurotic than their parents, secure within their limitations, though these are often marked'.[14] The most notable feature, though, is the deep peer attachments that they feel and the intensity of group ties. They function and experience the world better in their group than alone; they are reluctant to contemplate a life apart from each other. Bettelheim says: 'all these seem to speak more of bondage than attachment'; but he concludes: 'if intense group ties discourage individuation, neither do they breed human isolation, asocial behaviour or other forms of social disorganizations that plague modern man in competitive society'.[15] We might add that even the 'successes' of the individual child-rearing system may be less suited to a truly social life than the products of the kibbutz.

Communal societies like the Israeli kibbutzim often discourage an overemphasis on the obligations and attachments of the family. In many kibbutzim, husbands and wives are not allowed to work together and people are expected to refer to their parents, brothers and sisters and so on by their names rather than in the terminology of kinship. Similar principles informed many Christian communities in nineteenth-century America. The Oneida community, founded in New York State

[13] London 1969.
[14] Ibid, p. 261.
[15] Ibid., p. 262.

in 1848, consciously rejected the family and marriage as being inimical to a full communal life. The biblical text, 'In heaven they neither marry nor are given in marriage', was taken as justification for 'complex marriage' in which all the men and women of the community were joined. Heterosexual relations between any of them were encouraged; long-term pairing was discouraged. Children were cared for in a children's house soon after they were weaned, visiting their own parents only once or twice a week. Their founder John Humphrey Noyes saw a very clear contradiction between intense family feelings and community feeling. He believed that 'the great problem of socialism now is, whether the existence of the marital family is compatible with that of the universal family, which the term "community" signifies.'[16]

The Oneida community adhered to these principles for little longer than thirty years. The kibbutzim, too, have tended to strengthen family ties and give more time and space to family life as they have moved from the pioneering to a more established phase. In both cases the shift represents a retreat from socialist ideals, in the kibbutz case partly associated with the complexities of Israeli, Middle Eastern and world politics; in the Oneida case – the community actually became a joint stock company in 1881 – clearly and directly linked to hostile pressures from the locality and legal action against the community initiated by the Presbyterian Church. The fact that such experiments have not endured, or that they have become weakened and diluted, does not detract from the fact that they illustrate vividly how the strengthening of the community enables and requires the weakening of family ties.

These ideas were the commonplace of an earlier English tradition of socialist thought.[17] They have sadly faded from view. A vigorous critique of marriage was to be found in the writings of many early feminists. Yet it is often thought that the aspects of marriage they inveighed against have now disap-

[16] Noyes, *History of American Socialisms*, New York 1870, quoting Charles Lane.
[17] Barbara Taylor, 'The Woman-power: Religious Heresy and Feminism in Early English Socialism', in Susan Lipschitz, ed., *Tearing the Veil*, London 1978.

peared. Marriage is no longer so obviously the main source of livelihood available to bourgeois women – by which they were destined to 'the housekeeping trade', as Cecily Hamilton put it.[18] The campaigns for easier divorce, supported often by socialists and feminists, have meant that marriage is no longer so indissoluble that people are stuck for life in loveless or brutal bonds. The wedding ceremony itself has been modernized so that women no longer need promise to 'obey' or men to 'worship'. Shorn of its more obviously oppressive features, it is often thought that marriage is now a harmless or neutral institution. Yet this is far from being the case. The new marriage is seen as being both romantic and companionate – an impossible fusion, some would say – certainly a less stable form than the older, overtly male-dominated and more prosaic tie. It still produces couples who have a mystic bond, whose relationship is accepted as something special and beyond question. They easily slip into living as a social duo, each the 'better half' of the other, each only a half person, and often in a state of hostile dependency, resentful over the failings of a partner who is essential to them. Perhaps all couple relationships have this tendency, but marriage dignifies, privileges and romanticizes the couple.

The marriage relationship becomes protected from criticism, so that people are expected to put up with a great deal more from their spouse than they ever would from anyone else. An extreme example is the fact that there is, in the eyes of the law, no such thing as rape in marriage. A woman cannot refuse sex to her husband, though she should to every other man. The other side of the coin is that relationships outside the marriage become thinner and less meaningful. Men frequently have no intimate friends apart from their wife. The partners are expected to be loyal to each other if there is any conflict, so much so that a woman's relationship with her best friend or even a sister may be ruptured if their husbands do not get on. When a marriage breaks up – and it is the essence of the new marriage that it may well do so – the partners often find

[18] *Marriage as a Trade*, London 1909.

themselves friendless and isolated. A second marriage, replicating the first, is the easiest solution, and so a pattern of serial monogamy is set up. We have already discussed the appeal of such relationships. They do offer a promise of security and a resolution of many tensions and anxieties. Yet we must ask: if people need a long-term couple relationship, why do they get it sanctified by church, state and the most backward-looking elements of society? The cynical answer used to be that it was a good way of binding someone to you (though there was an odds-on chance that *you* would be bound unwillingly to *them*). The history of the struggle between state and church for control over marriage is not an edifying one, but it can at least teach us that marriage is a contract controlled not by the partners themselves but by the state. Furthermore it is an unwritten contract, one whose full implications become apparent only when divorce or separation (or, to some extent, death) lay bare its skeleton to public view and make clear that it is a contract not only about the sexual fidelity, cohabitation and mutual support mentioned in the wedding ceremony but also: sexual availability at will, housework, financial support even after marriage breakdown, a relation between a citizen head-of-household and a secondary dependant – and so on to indeterminate terms. We need not be in principle opposed to social control and concern in private household arrangements to believe that marriage is the wrong form for this.

Marriage is a form that is sanctified by tradition, not justified by rational social debate. The tradition is one that carries with it the whole historical baggage of male power and patriarchal authority. One has only to think of the traditional wedding ceremony, with its symbolic 'giving away' of the bride by her father to her husband, the white wedding-dress symbolizing her claim to virginity (or the cream one admitting that she cannot make this claim – though it will not show up in the photographic record), the striking contrast between men's and women's clothing in the wedding party.[19] But most important,

[19] Diana Leonard Barker, 'A Proper Wedding', in Marie Corbin, ed., *The Couple*, Harmondsworth 1978.

marriage is a form that conflates the sexual with the economic: as Engels so crisply pointed out, monogamous marriage and prostitution were born in the same moment.

Marriage, perhaps, represents a contradiction in the conservative confusion of individualism with familism. For if marriage is the basis of the family, then this supposedly individual and freely chosen form has a state instrument at its heart. Those who defend marriage as what people want and need must explain then why it has to be so massively privileged by social policy, taxation, religious endorsement and the accolade of respectability.

3. Privacy as Imprisonment

The exclusion of outsiders and turning in to the little family group may seem attractive when it works well and when the family does satisfy its members' needs. But the little enclosed group can also be a trap, a prison whose walls and bars are constructed of the ideas of domestic privacy and autonomy. Why is it that when a man is brutally assaulting his wife the police and neighbours – all of us – are so reluctant to intervene? It is thought of as interfering in a private matter. The bond between them is seen as so special that outsiders should not presume to take a stand, even when it is quite clear that what is happening is an extreme form of physical violence. Why is it that the woman in this situation is so reluctant to go to others for help or protection? She often accepts that violence is a normal risk of marriage or that *she* has failed in some way by inviting violence or not managing to stave it off.

The privacy of the family is cast in a new light if we realize that one quarter of reported violent crime is wife assault,[20] and that a very large proportion of rapes are carried out by men who know their victims well, often husbands, boyfriends, fathers and uncles.[21] If these are reported cases of violence and

[20] R.E. and R.P. Dobash, 'Wives: the "Appropriate" Victims of Marital Violence', *Victimology*, 2, 1977–78, pp. 426–42.
[21] *Rape Crisis Centre Report*, London 1977.

rape, we can safely assume that there is a huge penumbra of unreported incidents. It is ironical that the very expectations of security and protection in the private family are what make women so vulnerable to victimization within it, and so deprived of any recourse or plausible appeal to anyone outside its walls. Women often avoid going out alone at night for fear of being followed or attacked. Thus they become more ensnared in a home that may itself become a place of danger for them.

The recent public interest in domestic violence, spurred on by feminists, has produced a small increase in official willingness to intervene, and also improved legal procedures enabling a woman to obtain an injunction to exclude a violent man from the home. But it is apparent that for most women in such situations there is no solution other than actually leaving and breaking up the home. For a woman with children this is difficult to accomplish and even to contemplate. The existence now of a network of refuges for battered women, and the fact that local authorities are now obliged to provide accommodation for women with children who have left their home because of domestic violence can help women with some of the most pressing practical problems.[22] The difficulty of finding alternative housing is one of the solid walls of the little family prison, but other less tangible walls will keep many women from escaping.

Violence and rape, it may be thought, are not the everyday experience of family life for most people. This is probably true, though they are much commoner than roseate social images allow. But they do show up in a stark way how vulnerable people can be within the family. And they show how women are trapped much more than men. It is true that men sometimes experience the family as a mental prison, but they usually have far more opportunities for steering clear of the house if they want to. It is true that children can be beaten and psychologically confined and mistreated, but they too usually have an

---

[22] A useful discussion of recent developments is Val Binney, 'Domestic Violence: Battered Women in Britain in the 1970s', in the Cambridge Women's Studies Group, *Women in Society: Interdisciplinary Essays*, London 1981.

escape and another life of school and peers outside the home. It is women, whose work and emotional satisfaction is expected to centre around home and family, who are most fully imprisoned there.[23] The daily regime in the prison is not the drama of violence or rape, it is long hours of working banged up in a solitary cell while the guards attend to other, more important business. It is the mundane stuff of cartoons: it is 5.45 p.m. in a block of council flats. In each of fifty boxes a woman is frying the children's fish fingers, bathing the baby, putting the dirty clothes into the washing machine and peeling the potatoes for the husband's tea. All the same, but all in isolation. Even if she goes out to work, a woman must spend many hours on housework, and it is many hours of socially unrewarding work because it is not shared, is unrelieved by companionship.

It is not the character of the household tasks themselves that is oppressive, but the solitary, continuing and unrelieved nature of the multiplicity of household responsibilities. Many women will push their toddlers miles to a once-a-week play group just in order to have an hour alone without the child's constant questions and demands. The most common complaint of those who have to care for the senile or the severely disabled is that they *never* have any time off. Add to this the fact that the workplace is also the home, so that there is no separate leisure that is not intruded upon by the evidence of uncompleted tasks and the experience of enclosure is total. Of course most women also work outside the home for much of their lives, and others do manage to form bonds and interests outside it. But even so, they are usually more enmeshed in the family than men and are far more likely to be the ones who take the domestic responsibilities. It is they rather than men who give up their jobs while children are babies or when old people need to be cared for.

There are two striking, though crude, statistical facts that demand explanation. One is that far more men than women are

[23] See Annike Snäre and Tove Steng-Dahl, 'The Coercion of Privacy', Carol Smart and Barry Smart, eds., *Women, Sex and Social Control*, London 1978.

convicted of criminal offences; another is that more women than men are treated for depressive and neurotic mental illnesses. Though the processes involved are far from clear, it is hard to resist the conclusion that these correlations are in some way rooted in men's and women's different relation to private and public life. Men are more fully located in the public sphere and more fully challenge and fall foul of its formal techniques of social control. Women, on the other hand, are subjected to 'the coercion of privacy'[24] and are protected to some extent from the rigours of the criminal law. The processes of the behaviours and experiences of mental illness and of its diagnosis and treatment are much more complex than the criminal processes. It would be simplistic to describe them as 'social control', which implies that the behaviours labelled as mentally ill are free expressions of individual variety and the psychiatric procedures merely techniques for curbing and reducing to conformity.[25] It would be simplistic also to see becoming mentally ill just as a measure of suffering. Yet we do need to explain why women who work outside the home and unmarried women are less likely to become depressed than the housebound wife.[26] It is clear that being a housewife can drive women mad, though why they tend so often to experience depression and 'nerves' rather than, say, anger or revolt is perhaps less clear.

4. 'Women's Work'

After a decade of modern feminism, it is a commonplace to see women's association with housekeeping and child-care one of the keys to their oppression. The 'role differentiation' beloved of sociologists of the 1950s is nothing other than a very unequal division of labour. With the role of wife and mother goes

[24] Ibid.
[25] See L.J. Jordanova, 'Mental Illness, Mental Health: Changing Norms and Expectations', in Cambridge Women's Studies Group, pp. 95–114.
[26] Hannah Gavron, *The Captive Wife: Conflicts of Housebound Mothers*, Harmondsworth 1966.

housework. It is hard and exacting work. Ann Oakley's study of housewives with young children showed that they worked an average of 77 hours per week, including shopping and child-care but not including time spent relaxing in the house. The hours they worked ranged from 48 (this woman had a full-time paid job as well) to 105 per week.[27] Labour-saving equipment and ready-prepared food and clothing are not bringing about a reduction in these hours; they seem just to raise the standards of what must be done. With a freezer and a micro-wave oven, there is no excuse for a quick fry-up when you get home from work.

On the whole, women define housework as real work, and they do not enjoy it, or at best feel ambivalent about it. The major sources of dissatisfaction Ann Oakley found were that the work is monotonous repetitive and fragmented. It is made up of many different tasks, and although caring for children and cooking are fairly satisfying, many of the other tasks are not. Keeping a house clean and caring for children seem to contradict each other. Housewives work long hours at a pressurized pace. The work is done in lonely isolation from other adults. Housework has low status and even the families for whom it is done seem unappreciative, though they complain if the house is uncomfortable, their clothes not clean, their meals not ready, or if the woman has not time to give them her attention.[28]

The tasks are oppressive enough in themselves, especially when they must be performed in the isolated family. But most oppressive is the apparent inevitability with which women are destined to this vocation whether or nor they have a paid job and even whether or not they marry or have children. Women's consignment to housework does not even depend on marriage and financial support. Many old and disabled people have a female relative – a daughter, a niece, a mother – to keep house for them and look after them. The social services department is reluctant to take much responsibility if there is a woman they

[27] Ann Oakley, *The Sociology of Housework*, London 1974, p. 92.
[28] Ibid.; see also Oakley, *Housewife*, London 1974.

can foist it on. In myriad ways, the policies of the state services and of state income maintenance provisions assume and insist that women are destined to housework and to caring for those in need.[29] Underlying this is the assumption that to keep house is a natural adjunct of femininity. Wielding a needle or a mop, changing a nappy or a bed, not running out of flour or into debt come easily to women, it seems. We are blamed if we cannot manage them, whereas men are praised if they can. Girls are thought unnatural if they do not want to learn these skills as children; boys are thought unusual, if not unnatural, if they do. The natural association of women with housework is thought to be rooted in motherhood. The biological facts of childbearing and lactation lead, with an inevitability so obvious that it does not need to be spelled out, to primary responsibility for child-care, to a close intimate, warm bond between mother and infant, which extends naturally to buying and preparing its food, washing its clothes, binding its wounds, helping with its homework, taking it to the dentist, discussing its teenage problems, welcoming its husband or wife, grand-mothering its children. Enough has been written about the myth of motherhood to convince us that the reason those obvious and natural links do not need to be spelled out is that they would come apart if examined too closely.[30] The problem for women is not so much the tyranny of reproduction that Shulamith Firestone wished to overthrow (that can be tamed if we can control the technology); the problem is rather the tyranny of motherhood.

This may sound an extraordinary thing to say when many women clearly wish and choose to become mothers. What they can seldom choose, though, are the social circumstances and pressures that would enable them to resist being swamped by motherhood. There is often such a tension between being a mother and being whatever else you want to be that neither can

---

[29] Hilary Land, 'Who Cares for the Family?', *Journal of Social Policy*, vol. 7, part 3, 1978; Elizabeth Wilson, *Women and the Welfare State*.

[30] An early summary is Ann Oakley, *Sex, Gender and Society*, London 1972, pp. 128–36.

be fully enjoyed. Sometimes women who would really like to have children decide not to because they cannot work out a social situation in which they can do so without giving up everything else. Many women do give up their paid work and other projects. Usually they find their relationship with their children deeply rewarding; but at the same time they feel frustrated that it has become such an exclusive and demanding one. All too often, in the context of the isolated private family, and with little outside support, motherhood becomes a burden in itself and also a major means by which women become trapped in the home. Even couples who at first share the cooking and cleaning equally seldom do so after the children arrive. The woman stays at home to care for the small baby, so obviously she takes care of the running of the house at the same time. Later, if she returns to outside work she does a 'double shift'. The man has to earn enough to support the whole family, so obviously he has not much time or energy left for domestic matters. Gradually the knots linking the woman to the home and family become tightened. If she is lucky she may find it rewarding; if she does not she is unlucky. Most likely, though, she feels deeply ambivalent about it because it is her love for her children that ties her down. This is what we mean by the tyranny of motherhood.

Men, on the other hand, can usually choose how and how much they get involved with their children. They are expected to take some part, but also to be the outside authority and final arbiter. Many of them play with their children a good deal in their spare time, but seldom do they carry the regular responsibility of physical and emotional care.

It is often said that men do a great deal about the house as well. They put up shelves and repair things that go wrong; they see to the car (which thereby becomes *their* car, if it was not already); they look after the bank account and the mortgage. But all the chores that men do can be done by women and often are, whereas there are many elements of housework that a man will seldom do if there is a woman around to do them. Often these are the tasks that are considered undignified. Surveys in which men and women are asked about what tasks they perform in and around the home typically show that men claim to do more things than women say they do. In general, men's jobs have more of a voluntary character. Do-it-yourself work is often even seen as a hobby; it can be done as and when the man chooses. His contributions to the routine chores that go to make up housework are often seen as 'helping' his wife. The work properly belongs to her, but he will help her out if he has time and if he wants to. For her, the tasks are seen as inescapable; for him they are not. Women's commitment to housework is not imposed on them by their own menfolk in a straightforward way. Indeed many men would not notice whether the house was clean and tidy or not, provided their meals were ready on time and their clothes washed for them. One of the great problems of the politics of housework is the question of standards: the chief immediate reason that women do most of it is that they are brought up to be more attuned to cleanliness and more anxious about dirt and mess. Researchers who have interviewd housewives have been struck by two things above all. One was how dissatisfied they were with their lot,[31] the other was their obsessive approach to their work. Lee Comer commented that for the housewives she talked to, 'almost every one felt obliged to apologize for "the state" their homes were in, even when they were immaculate'.[32] She suggests that they often submit to real or imagined external moral pressure from other women because this is the only way of giving housework any rationality. Since the housewife's work is in fact so private, 'if she insists on satisfying only her own requirements in a wholly utilitarian way, she risks being labelled self-indulgent and immoral'.[33]

Women's exaggeratedly high standards for housework are not just a product of their own life situation. They are also

[31] Lee Comer wrote: 'I expected to hear complaints, but I never dreamed for a moment I would encounter so much sadness, bitterness and disillusion' (*Wedlocked Women*, Leeds 1974, p. 280).
[32] Ibid., p. 92; Ann Oakley (*Housewife*), also notes the obsessional nature of much housework.
[33] *Woman's Own*, 1975.

passed on from one generation to another. Historically they were created and reinforced by schools, domestic science propaganda and social workers; today they are stimulated by the media, especially in advertising. The endless proliferation of separate little households has been an ideal ally in the constant capitalist effort to expand consumption and keep up the demand for ever more commodities. The woman, as the moving spirit of each household, needs to be deeply concerned with its physical state, its equipment, its style. She is acutely aware of how it compares with other households in her milieu; her aim is that it should replicate them while being slightly better in some respects. If she can accomplish this she serves not only the economic needs of capital, but also helps to produce an apparently uniform population which seems more divided by competition, envy and life-style than by the struggle of classes.

Any struggle to end the division of labour in the family, to get men to share in the routine household cares, involves converting men from idle parasitism and presumed incapacity. But it also involves breaking out of the dead-end of the 'it's easier to do it myself' mentality. This mentality, premissed as it is on the acceptance that it is women's work and women know how best it should be done, even when done by men, invites passive resistance and even dumb insolence from the men who have never been permitted to establish the goals or agree the means for this new shared activity. Yet this mentality is not arbitrary; it cannot be abandoned by a mere effort of will. For one thing, it is genuinely true that housework, cooking and child-care are complex activities in which most women have been fully and thoroughly trained over a lifetime. Though their attitude may be sometimes obsessional, the rules that they apply are usually rational and well-founded in experience. Furthermore, women's emotional investment in housework is a product of a situation in which marriage, family and home-making are usually the most promising career available. For most young women, the cards are heavily stacked in favour of becoming a wife. As they say: 'It's easy for a woman to get the same pay as a man – all she has to do is marry one.'

The apparently indissoluble link between femininity and keeping house and looking after people is thus rooted in the family, but extends well beyond its confines. To challenge the division of labour in the family would be to challenge an oppressive feature of the femininity that is so limiting to women.

5. Petty Power and Social Power

The division of labour in the family is associated with the greater power of men. Despite the contemporary rhetoric of the 'egalitarian family' and the 'sharing marriage', despite the disappearance of the more obvious formalized manifestations of paternal power and manly authority, modern families are still deeply unequal affairs. The principle of the wage-earner and his dependants, of the husband who contributes cash while the wife contributes household labour, is not a division of labour between equals, but an unequal exchange in which the man's interests predominate.

Even if we ignore, for the moment, the more intangible things like authority, self-esteem, deference and submission, and look only at the almost-measurable distribution of goods and services in the household, it is clear that (1) the man's benefit from the housework that women do is far more than equivalent to the support that he gives her, (2) such support is very variable and its extent is conditional upon good will, and (3) decisions about shared consumption often work in favour of the things that men want.

(1) If the cash value of a wife's multifarious services (on the open market) were computed it would far exceed what a husband could afford to pay. A recent survey found that the average housewife is fully employed for seven days a week (though Sunday is a fairly light day with only six-and-a-half hours work). If she were paid at the going rate for each of her various activities, from cost clerk, through waitress, laundress and childminder, to cleaner, her salary would be £204 a week,

or £10,600 a year.[34] Even a comparison of the hours and conditions of work of wives with those of living-in general servants (whom most men could not begin to afford) shows that men are getting an extremely good bargain out of the support they offer.

But even if men who supported their wives entirely could be said to pay fairly for the benefits they received, this could hardly be said in the much commoner cases where the wife also earns some money and contributes it towards household expenses. If she earns a wage that is half of her husband's, she raises their total joint income and also relieves him of half of what he previously paid for her support. Yet the amount of housework that she does is not reduced by anything like as much as a half.

Household services are very different from commodities and the terms on which men obtain their wives' services are very different from those of the market-place. The question of exchange is seldom an overt one. Men may pay their children to clean their car or run an errand, but they do not pay their wives to clean the living room or make them a cup of tea. Households formed on the basis of kinship are the only setting in which such free domestic services are available, provided on the basis of the love and duty associated with kinship and marriage. It seems almost sacrilegious to intrude economic calculation into the bosom of the family, conducted as it is on affectional and not economic principles. Yet if, when we do so, our calculations reveal gross inequities, we can see that, like many sacred mysteries, the mystic bonds of family serve to mask mundane exploitation.

(2) Do men really share their incomes, as the ideal model of marriage would suggest? A growing amount of evidence shows that they seldom do, and that there is little their wives can do about it. The ways in which families organize their internal financial arrangements are so varied that it is hard to state any

[34] Survey by Gallup Poll for Legal and General Assurance, *The Times*, 11 November 1981.

general rules about them, but the very fact of this variety might suggest that husbands have a good deal of say in deciding just how much they will share.

An arrangement that used to be very widespread among working-class people in Britain and is still quite common in Scotland and the North of England, especially where the wife has no income and the husband's income is low, is the one known as 'tipping up'.[35] Under this system, the husband (and formerly any working sons and daughters living at home) hands over his whole wage packet to the wife and gets given his pocket money, normally a fixed amount. This is often held up as evidence of a sound working-class tradition of sharing, yet in fact it ensures that the wage-earner gets money for purely personal spending, while the housewife gets only what is needed for the common household expenses.

The other well-known and apparently very widespread system is where the wife is given a housekeeping allowance, a standard weekly amount to cover all the household expenditure. The rest of his income is the man's to spend as he wishes, while she must either save out of the housekeeping or ask him for money for anything she wants for herself. This system seems calculated to maximize bad feeling and resentment. A man with a variable pay-packet may find his pocket-money much reduced in some weeks. The woman finds that the amount she is allowed does not go up with rising prices. She often may not know how much her husband earns, and there is evidence that increases in his pay are often not reflected in increased housekeeping money.[36]

Men whose wages are paid into the bank instead of in cash often take over responsibility for some of the household expenditure, paying the larger bills for rent or mortgage payments and often gas and electricity. The housekeeping allowance then only has to cover smaller cash outlays. Indeed,

---

[35] J.E. Todd and L.M. Jones, *Matrimonial Property* (OPCS Survey for the Law Commission), London 1972; A. Gray, 'The Working-Class Family as an Economic Unit', unpublished doctoral thesis, University of Edinburgh 1974.

[36] *Woman's Own*, 1975.

supermarkets have made possible an arrangement where the weekly shopping is done by the couple together and paid for by the man with his cheque-book – in extreme cases he need give his wife no cash at all.[37]

The worst aspect of all these ways of managing money is that they fuse the interests of women with those of the family. Children have pocket-money, men have pocket-money, or else the residue of their wage, but women have only the money destined for housekeeping. Everything she spends 'on herself' is taken out of what could have gone on food or on clothes for the children. In fact, until 1964 anything she saved out of the housekeeping allowance legally belonged to the husband. Now it belongs to both equally, though most people are not aware of this.[38] And, whatever the law may say, there is something very ambiguous about such savings, given the ideology that Ann Whitehead has called 'maternal altruism', in which the mother always puts 'the family' or 'the children' first and gets her satisfaction from spending on them and not on herself.[39] Expenditure on herself is supposed to induce guilt: she buys a new dress to 'cheer herself up', whereas a working man needs his fares and his cigarette and drink money to help him through the working day.

(3) A complete pooling of resources is clearly the most progressive and egalitarian arrangement. Wages or salaries are paid into a joint bank account, or put into a joint purse, from which all expenditures, whether common or personal, are made. Of the housewives she interviewed for *The Captive Wife*[40] Hannah Gavron found that 56% of wives of 'middle-class' men and 77% of wives of 'working-class' men had only a regular allowance to manage on. So sharing seems to be a more

---

[37] Jan Pahl, 'Patterns of Money Management Within Marriage' *Journal of Social Policy*, vol. 9, part 3, 1980, p. 326.

[38] Todd and Jones, p. 31.

[39] '"I'm Hungry, Mum"': The Politics of Domestic Budgeting', Kate Young, Carol Wolkowitz and Roslyn McCullagh, eds., *Of Marriage and Markets*, London 1981, p. 107.

[40] London 1966.

frequent pattern among white collar workers, though interestingly it is followed more where both partners are earning, rather than only the man. Yet in this apparently equal situation, everything depends upon how spending decisions are made. In practice, the decision-making power lies with the one who brings in the sole or major income. In any marriage relationship, practical and emotional considerations are all mixed up together, but the outcome is usually clear. The fact that the husband actually earns his money is important, even where couples pool their resources. Where they do not, it is common for the husband's earnings to cover things that are thought of as 'necessary' expenditures, such as rent, heating, normal food buying and regular outgoings which cannot readily be reduced, while the wife's are spent on things thought of as 'extras'.[41] This practice may be rational in the sense that the couple need to be sure that they could manage on the husband's income, since the wife's is much more insecure, but it also has the effect of reinforcing the idea of the breadwinner-and-dependant even when the wife is not fully dependent. In fact, of course, the 'pin money' is not for personal fripperies but goes towards maintaining the family's standard of living: many families would fall below the poverty line without the wife's earnings.

Goodwill and a progressive outlook are not enough to work away the power differential that comes from the fact of women's dependence. In a society where 'supporting yourself' is equated with 'earning an income', contributing to the household on an unpaid basis can never give the woman the same rights as the man. Furthermore, unless *he* has the goodwill and the progressive outlook she will be completely at his mercy.

We do not wish to suggest that the man's domination in the family is simply a product of the economic imbalance in the particular case. If this were so, the strategy for correcting it could rely entirely on getting women out into employment on

[41] Pauline Hunt, 'Cash Transactions and Household Tasks: Domestic Behaviour in Relation to Industrial Employment', *Sociological Review*, vol. 26, no. 3, 1978, p. 569.

an equal basis with men. This was the view of Engels, who argued that the entry of women into industrial production would eliminate the economic inequality between working-class women and men and so abolish the basis for the subordination of women. History since his day has proved that men have been able to establish a sexual division of labour in industrial production and between industry and family, and so to prevent the very fact of capitalist industrial employment from becoming the great leveller that Engels anticipated. Men have successfully fought for the rather more privileged job situations, leaving the insecure and low-paid work to women and immigrant workers. Even when women do go out to full-time jobs their pay is on average only a percentage of men's. But men have also allowed 'full-time work' to become so defined that it is hard to combine with any household responsibilities. The hours and conditions of employment are usually such that the worker has no right to time off for shopping, to care for a sick child, to stay in for the washing-machine repairer or any of the hundred-and-one exigencies of domestic life, so the petty power that men wield in the family is backed up by their power in the wider social world.

The experience of many women has also proved that even when two partners in a marriage bring in similar incomes the man retains his domination in all sorts of non-economic ways. The structures of domination and submission go far beyond the material facts of providing and dependence, into the unconscious, into sexuality, into all the rituals of love, cosiness, deference, cajoling, leadership, that go to make up the daily interactions between wives and husbands. The practice of consciousness raising in the Women's Liberation Movement has uncovered many subtle, taken-for-granted ways in which men dominate and women submit. Some of the most disturbing of these are the forms of collusion in our own oppression that we all adopt. Women's guilt, lack of self-confidence, willingness to get something by charm if they can't get it as of right, all play into the hands of men's power.

6. Sexual Liberation

The unequal power in marriage lies at the root of an imbalance between men's and women's sexuality that is becoming more and more contested. Heterosexual relations between adults, modelled on the procreative act, are privileged above all other forms of sexual expression. Monogamy is morally endorsed. Science and folklore concur in the belief that men have positive and often aggressive sexual drives, which are often promiscuous rather than directed towards one mate, while women's sexual interests are weaker and more diffuse, part of the emotional expression of a deep relationship and responsive to the man's desires rather than self-generating. It is even believed that women's sexuality is more closely bound up with conception and motherhood, though there is no biological basis for this belief: on the contrary women's sexual pleasure has no procreative function whereas the man's orgasm in intercourse is necessary to conception.

Feminists have always recognized the gross asymmetry of the 'double standard' of morality, which condones male philandering while enjoining chastity for women, as a form of male privilege. It degrades women by encouraging prostitution; it makes other women forever the objects of male advances that they must forever repel. In the nineteenth century, feminists most often saw sex as a primitive urge that all civilized people should strive to control. It wasted energy and health, spread venereal disease and brought unwanted children, as well as degrading women. So they celebrated rather than deplored the asexual idea of womanhood. The solution, that men should curb their bestial impulses, had its most succinct, if extreme, expression in Christabel Pankhurst's slogan: 'votes for women and chastity for men'.[42]

In early socialist thought in England there had been another tradition, fed by the streams of Robert Owen's utopianism and the historical materialism of Marx and Engels. Both saw the

---

[42] *The Great Scourge*, London 1913. Early feminist views on sexuality are discussed in Jeffrey Weeks, *Sex, Politics and Society; The Regulation of Sexuality Since 1800*, London 1981, pp. 160–7.

72

existing forms of sexuality as a product of social arrangements. Marx wrote that the sexual relation of men and women 'reveals the extent to which man's *natural* behaviour has become *human*. . . the extent to which he in his individual existence is at the same time a social being.'[43] Utopianism contributed a lively critique of the constraints of monogamy, especially in its inegalitarian forms, and a shining vision of a socialism in which people's lives would be guided by self-determination rather than the externally imposed laws of church and state. Historical materialism contributed the belief that each historic era has its own way of life and form of family. Engels argued that private property was associated with male dominance, monogamy and the indissolubility of marriage. Monogamy he saw as desirable, provided it was cut free of its economic mooring, but he expected socialism to bring the equality of the sexes and the freedom to leave a dead union and form another one.[44]

Though some socialists played a part in the sex reform movement in the early years of this century and in the movement for birth control, sexual libertarianism has not been a dominant strand in English socialist thought. Indeed, George Ives commented in 1904 that: 'There is a curious kind of "Socialism" in this country, which is allied with Christianity and even with Grundyism. That, to my mind, is more hateful than the present order. The socialism to which I belong, and to which solid millions adhere on the Continent, refuses all compromises with the religious parties, all compromises with existing sexual morality, all compromises with the class system in any shape.'[45] For the most part, the politics of sexuality has remained outside the mainstream, marginalized by a general consensus that questions of sex are concerned with morality and private life and not with the big issues of power

[43] *Economic and Philosophical Manuscripts of 1844*, Moscow n.d., p. 101, quoted by Jeffrey Weeks, *Sex, Politics and Society*, where there is an interesting discussion of socialist ideas on sexuality (pp. 167–75).
[44] *The Origin of the Family, Private Property and the State*.
[45] Letter to Janet Ashbee, 15 February 1904: *Ashbee Journals*, King's College, Cambridge. Quoted in Weeks, p. 167.

and economics. It is this consensus that the new Women's Liberation Movement has sought to destroy, with the slogan 'the personal *is* political' and a nagging insistence on raising questions about violence, sex, abortion, contraception on what were previously the most inappropriate occasions, like trade union meetings and May Day celebrations. But although the Women's Liberation Movement is united on the importance of these questions, there is much less certainty about where the answers lie. Some favour an all-out attack on pornography, more effective punishment of sexual molesters and rapists, and even women's withdrawal from all heterosexual relations. Others, including ourselves, believe that no solution to our sexual malaise is possible without a more fundamental transformation in the power relation between women and men. On the other hand, we are more optimistic than many about the possibilities of ameliorating human nature, even including the sexual nature of men.

The sex reform movement of this century has brought enormous benefits. Few people are as ignorant about sex as they were in the nineteenth century. Knowledge of birth control and of venereal diseases makes sex more enjoyable. The challenging of taboos means that people feel less guilty about masturbation and about homosexuality. Women's sexual pleasure is better understood and is seen as a good thing. Many even believe that all the restrictions and hang-ups of Victorian sexuality have been swept away in the tide of permissiveness and that sex is now frank and free and truly mutual.

Yet, how fundamental a change has there really been? A gross asymmetry in heterosexual relations remains, despite these improvements. Men still seek and are willing to pay for the services of prostitutes, often asking for the fulfilment of the most bizarre fantasies and fetishes. They pour huge sums of money into the burgeoning trade of pornographic magazines, pictures, films and video-tapes which represent women as the objects of male desire. Clubs, pubs and conferences of businessmen and union men are routinely entertained with girly strip-shows. Men still rape women. Fathers still commit incest with their daughters. It is practically never the other way round. This asymmetry in sex is still as great as it ever was, much greater than in many supposedly primitive societies. Women are no longer expected to be chaste, but sex is still on men's terms. It is almost as if women's obvious sexual enjoyment were just another thing that men can demand of them. A far cry from the feminist dream of autonomy, from being a sexual agent rather than a sexual object, it turns out that a 'liberated lady' is more fun in bed – for the man. The weakening of the rigid rules has only added to the anxieties of growing up for girls. They still see a social danger in being too much available to boys sexually, they still fear that being too little available will mean they are ignored by boys. The polarity between the slag and the drag, between the girl who sleeps around and the nice girl who doesn't, has a long history.[46] In the nineteenth century it was the virgin and the whore, the madonna and the magdalen, the respectable woman and the fallen woman.[47] At the same time, even among the respectable, girls had to be wary of flirting or being fast. The boundary has shifted a good deal since then. In most circles, girls can sleep with one boyfriend if it is a steady relationship and they are in love. The stakes have risen, but the game has basically the same rules: men pressurize women into going too far and then despise them for it. Women's main concern must always be not with what they want themselves, but with how to strike just the right balance in attracting or repelling men.

This sexual asymmetry is social rather than natural in its origins.[48] It is part of the pattern of courtship and of marriage. In the long testing-time of youth, boys can afford to seek sexual enjoyment; they are expected to prove themselves as men. They may also be looking for someone to marry, someone who will settle with them, take care of their house and children. Chasing girls is both a search for pleasure and a way of testing girls out,

---

[46] Celia Cowie and Sue Lees, 'Slags or Drags', *Feminist Review*, no. 9, autumn 1981.

[47] Eric Trudgill, *Madonnas and Magdalens*, London 1976.

[48] Mary McIntosh, 'Who Needs Prostitutes? The Ideology of Male Sexual Needs', Carol Smart and Barry Smart, eds., *Women, Sexuality and Social Control*, London 1978. We have also discussed the way the idea of the natural is used in ideology in chapter 1.

sorting them into those who are alright for a good time and those who are more serious. For a girl, the need to marry is more serious. It is often the chief thing she looks forward to in the future. It will alter her whole life much more than it will her husband's life. Realistically, her chances of earning good money are lower, and marriage and dependence on a husband to supplement her income offer a better standard of living and more security than she could expect if she was single. So, early in life the girl feels she must regulate her sexual behaviour to serve this goal. The danger of being labelled a slag is the danger of not being taken seriously as a possible partner. She cannot afford to explore her own sexuality or develop her own desires for fear of losing her reputation and self-esteem. For her activity is always reinterpreted as receptivity. Her sexual achievements are not conquests but defeats; she is 'anybody's', an easy lay, the object of the man's desire. Her job is to defend herself, to ration her favours. She learns to parry advances, to tease, to feint, to gain a modicum of control in a situation where she is basically disadvantaged.

The fact that this whole pattern, degrading to all concerned, has survived intact through the great upheavals of the permissive age suggests that it is more than a mere relic of an outdated Victorian code. Deep-seated differences between the sexes do tend to be reproduced from generation to generation by the fact that children are reared by a pair of differentiated parents and the parameters of their sexual orientation are set in the context of their early relations with those parents.[49] But our unbalanced pattern of sexuality is also an integral part of a thriving marriage system that still enshrines male power and female dependence. Until that form of family disappears, sexual enjoyment will continue to be a male privilege and it will continue to take the form of sexual possession. Clearly, then, it remains necessary, as the early socialists recognized, to separate sex love from these economic ties and allow it to flourish in its own right.

[49] For psychoanalytic interpretations of the reproduction of femininity see Juliet Mitchell, *Psychoanalysis and Feminism*, London 1974; Nancy Chodorow, *The Reproduction of Mothering*, Berkeley, California 1978.

Defenders of the family commonly argue that we have only to look around us to see that sex outside of marriage is less satisfactory than sex within it. It is certainly true that prostitution, pornography, and sexualization of the mass media, many facets of the male gay scene and, as we have seen, the pre-marital sex of teenage years all reflect a predatory, dehumanized male sexuality. Yet they are so unpleasant because they are forbidden, rather than forbidden because they are unpleasant. Men would not be willing to pay prostitutes if it were not for the fact that their heterosexual desires have been indulged and accorded legitimacy and women's constructed as weak and receptive, in the interests of a male dominated marriage system. The same applies to pornography and the mass media. Homosexual life would not be so distinct and ghettoized if heterosexual marriage were not both inordinately privileged by social mores and also stressful and unattractive, so that many are willing to risk ridicule and ostracism rather than follow the conventional patterns. In milder forms, the polarity of active and passive, with its echoes of hunter and hunted, possessor and possessed, permeates almost all sexual relations, whether between women, between men or between women and men. No sexual relation can be entirely free from the pervasive imagery based on marriage. Yet it is also true that within marriage, and within other long-term pairs, it is sometimes possible to develop relations of sexual reciprocity and caring. But it would be wrong to conclude from this that the solution to modern sexual problems is to strengthen marriage and the family and try to confine sex to the domestic setting. For it is precisely the oppressive and unbalanced nature of the family that creates the kind of sexuality that exists outside it. Confining sex within marriage is not the answer to the problem; at the social level it is itself the cause of the problem.

7. Family Gains and Social Losses

What happens outside families is much affected by the

existence of the family as a privileged institution. Every other aspect of social life is planned on the assumption that people live in families. Those who do not are isolated and deprived. Spinsters, older batchelors and couples who do not have children are frowned upon; people who live by themselves are thought to be abnormal. The popular image of the family – the married couple living with their young children – is constantly projected as the image of normality and of happiness. Yet in fact half the population do not live in this situation. Even those who do get married and have children themselves spend only the first sixteen or so years of their lives and, say twenty years of adulthood living in a family with children. The bulk of their lives is spent living just with adults or on their own. In Britain in 1979, 23% of households had only one person, 27% had a married couple on their own, and only 31% had a married couple living with their dependent children.[50]

Yet the family ideal makes everything else seem pale and unsatisfactory. Those who live alone often suffer from loneliness. Families are so wrapped up in their little domestic life that they have not time to spend on visiting; their social life is with people like themselves. Couples mix with other couples, finding it difficult to fit single people in. The middle-class custom of balancing the sexes at dinner parties is only a formalized version of the endemic exclusion of the single, divorced and widowed. The estrangement of the sexes, outside of specifically sexual relationships, persists at all ages and increases isolation even among the elderly. The cosy image of the family makes all other settings where people can mix and live together seem like second-best. Nurseries, children's homes, student residences, nursing homes, old people's homes, all in their different ways conjure up pictures of bleakness, deprivation, acceptable perhaps for day care or for part of the year or a brief stage in life, but very much a *pis aller* to be resorted to only if normal family life cannot be provided. Hospital social workers expect a daughter, mother or wife to look after a discharged patient in preference to a convalescent home; nursery nurses are trained

50 Central Statistical Office, *Social Trends 11*, London 1981.

in the theories of John Bowlby and taught to believe a small child is better off spending all day with its mother; old people's homes are only for those who can no longer care for themselves and they are expected to give up most of their autonomy on entering. The old poor-law principle of 'less eligibility' whereby relief was only provided under conditions considerably less attractive than self-support seems to have been translated into a new sphere: living outside the family is possible, but only under conditions considerably less attractive than those within it. Yet it need not be so. Old people's homes could be a lot more like residential hotels, or else like self-governing communities. A home for the handicapped can be considerably more stimulating for a teenager with Down's syndrome than living alone with her parents. A nursery or children's home can provide positive social experiences of cooperation, companionship and varied activities. It is the over-valuation of family life that devalues these other lives. The family sucks the juice out of everything around it, leaving other institutions stunted and distorted.

Production and all paid work is organized to dovetail with a particular kind of family, one in which the wife is responsible for housekeeping and caring for the family members and can be dependent on the husband's income if need be. Any housewife or parent who has had an ordinary full-time job finds that work is planned at places and times that are incompatible with domestic responsibilities. The hours of work, the distance from shops, the problems of taking time off are all well enough suited to a man who has a wife at home taking care of the house and children, the shopping and cooking, staying in for the gas-meter reader, going out to the school sports day. So it is not surprising that so many women have part-time jobs when they do go out to work.[51] Nor is it surprising that there are probably approaching half a million women who work for money at home, doing machining, assembling, clerical work and child-minding. Because of their home responsibilities many women have a rather marginal

---

[51] 40.8°ₒ in the United Kingdom, compared with 2.3"ₒ for men, according to the EEC Labour Force Sample Survey, 1977, Table 12.

relation to the labour market. On the other hand, almost all women are disadvantaged in the labour market from the word go, and it is partly this that makes marriage an attractive option for them. If your chances of earning a good income are small (and women's average weekly earnings for full-time work are only 63% of men's)[52] dependence on a man, even if it involves household cares that further reduce your ability to earn, may seem a wise choice.

At first sight, then, there appears to be a neat fit between women's place in the labour market and their place at home. Their part-time or less permanent involvement in paid work frees them to run the home; men's full-time work enables them to earn a 'family wage' to support a dependent wife and children. Many would say that women are not disadvantaged in earning a living, but are able to earn in a way appropriate to their family position. 'It is normal for a married woman in this country to be primarily supported by her husband, and she looks to him for support when not actually working', was the way a minister in the Department of Health and Social Security put it.[53] Yet when we realize that this supposedly normal pattern of dependence is in fact a myth,[54] it becomes clear that the supposedly appropriate pattern of women having less training, fewer job opportunities and lower pay is nothing less than a con trick made possible by the power of the family myth. The trick is given another bitter twist when it is argued that since women now have equal rights at work, their husband no longer has the responsibility to maintain them. Such is the argument offered by the Campaign for Justice in Divorce in favour of abolishing the husband's obligation to maintain his wife after divorce.

So there is constructed a curious house of cards in which the myth and the reality of the family alternately provide support for ever more ramshackle and unsatisfactory excrescences, each of which in turn serves to shore up the myth and keep the

[52] *New Earnings Survey*, 1978, Part A.
[53] Brian O'Malley, letter to the Women's Liberation Campaign for Legal and Financial Independence, 1976.
[54] Hilary Land, 'The Myth of the Male Breadwinner', *New Society*, 9 October 1975.

reality more or less intact. The world around the family is not a pre-existing harsh climate against which the family offers protection and warmth. It is as if the family had drawn comfort and security into itself and left the outside world bereft. As a bastion against a bleak society it has made that society bleak. It is indeed a major agency for caring, but in monopolizing care it has made it harder to undertake other forms of care. It is indeed a unit of sharing, but in demanding sharing within it has made other relations tend to become more mercenary. It is indeed a place of intimacy, but in privileging the intimacy of close kin it has made the outside world cold and friendless, and made it harder to sustain relations of security and trust except with kin. Caring, sharing and loving would be more widespread if the family did not claim them for its own.

III

Contemporary Social Analysis

1. Deconstructing the Family

It is important to note an ambiguity in our expression 'the anti-social family'. Do we suggest that *the* family, recognizable in its different forms, is an essentially anti-social institution, or that this particular *type* of family is anti-social? In one sense there is a 'correct' answer to this question: we must refer to a particular, historically and socially specific, form of family since no general or essential category can be derived analytically from the many and varied arrangements commonly lumped together as the family. This is not a particularly original or revolutionary insight, but is widely accepted among historians and sociologists working on these questions. Michael Anderson, for instance, writes in the introduction to his beginner's guide to family history that 'the one unambiguous fact which has emerged in the last twenty years is that there can be no simple history of *the* Western family since the sixteenth century because there is not, nor ever has there been, a single family system. The West has always been characterized by diversity of family forms, by diversity of family functions and by diversity in attitudes to family relationships not only over time but at any one point in time. There is, except at the most trivial level, no Western family type'.[1] Anderson is of course right, but his statement is one that writers on the family usually find difficult to put into practice in the way they

[1] *Approaches to the History of the Western Family 1500-1914*, London 1980, p. 14.

conceptualize and present their material and interpretations. His own book, presumably, would have been more accurately entitled *Approaches to the Histories of Western Family Types 1500–1914* but such formulations are clumsily pedantic in tone and used infrequently.

Olivia Harris sees the problem as arising from the broader ideological significance of 'the family' to our culture and consciousness. She writes: 'Why then, given all we know about the variation in domestic arrangements, is it so common to find the domestic domain treated as a universal, or at least very widespread institution? Even those who recognize that the co-resident nuclear family is a historically specific idea will in the next breath talk of 'the' family, 'the' household in a way that surreptitiously reintroduces an assumption of universalism. Working as an anthropologist I have often noticed myself perform this same slippage and have wondered why it comes so easily. One explanation is that the image of the household as a separate, private sphere is so powerful in contemporary capitalist organization that we extend it to cover other radically different structures, using our own categories of thought to interpret different realities.'[2] When we look at 'the family' in detail we see that the naturalistic unit so widely referred to comprises many distinct elements, all of which may vary, such as kinship, marriage, sexuality, household size and organization, and so forth. Furthermore, the relationships between the sphere designated domestic and that seen as 'public' also vary from society to society.

Consideration of the social significance of family organization has been an important focus in sociology and anthropology, a central political concern of feminism, a recurring preoccupation in Marxism, and has generated a productive sub-field within historical research and analysis. These different standpoints understandably pose questions of varying kinds, and it is not to be expected that the answers can readily be compared systematically. Yet this alone does not explain the

[2] 'Households as Natural Units', in Kate Young, Carol Wolkowitz and Roslyn McCullagh, eds., *Of Marriage and the Market*, London 1981, pp. 50, 51.

contradictions, disagreements and confusions that strike the reader of these various treatments of 'family and society'. On virtually every fundamental point of fact, interpretation and analysis there is a complete lack of consensus. Each writer demonstrates an experiential certainty of the object under the microscope – the family – but the reader is left with the impression, from accumulated accounts, that they are simply not talking about the same thing.

To take an example within a specific perspective, that of family history as an academic discipline, we find that Anderson's position, quoted at the beginning of this chaper, is entirely denied by Peter Laslett. Far from endorsing the view that no single family form is characteristic of the West, Laslett maintains that, pending evidence to the contrary, we should assume that the nuclear form of the family prevails. He argues, on the basis of historical evidence that has been much discussed since the publication of his work, that departures from this family form are merely the 'fortuitous outcomes' of localized demographic, economic or personal factors. In his insistence that the extended family is no more than a sociological myth, Laslett puts forward the proposition that 'the present state of evidence forces us to assume that the family's organization was always and invariably nuclear, unless the contrary can be proven'.[3]

Anderson and Laslett are the most influential representatives of family history in Britain and it is for this reason that we draw attention to this basic difference as puzzling to the non-specialist reader. How can it be that one authority says there is no 'family type' of Western Europe while the other believes the evidence demonstrates incontrovertibly that such a generic form does exist?

In general terms, some of the difficulties in comparing different accounts of the family arise from the wide range of current meanings of the term. It is instructive to look at those specified in the OED, since the choice listed there makes for considerable variation and points to a need for rigorous

[3] *Household and Family in Past Time*, London 1972, pp. x, 73.

specification of what is at stake. Among the major meanings for the term – disregarding the obsolete ones that no doubt still colour usage – are:

1. The body of persons who live in one house or under one head, including parents, children, servants, etc.

2. The group of persons consisting of the parents and their children, whether actually living together or not; in a wider sense, the unity formed by those who are nearly connected by blood or affinity.

3. Those descended or claiming descent from a common ancestor; a house, kindred, lineage.

The adjective 'familiar' is listed as having the following meanings: pertaining to one's family or household, private, domestic, friendly, intimate, domesticated, well known, ordinary, usual, homely, plain, easily understood, unceremonious.[4]

In these definitions we see the fundamental ambiguity of the term 'family': does it refer to the members of a residential household or to people connected by ties of marriage and kinship? The French historian Jean-Louis Flandrin has argued that these two meanings were relatively separate in the past and that it was only in the nineteenth century that they became conflated, with the modern meaning of 'family' as co-residing close kin emerging as the dominant one.[5] There is obvious evidence, however, that this dominant meaning has not entirely carried the day in that the term 'family' still carries the connotations of the earlier different meanings. From the definition of family as household we have – leaving aside the rather archaic inclusion of servants – the idea that the family is the locus of all that is domestic, private, intimate, well known and unceremonious. From the definition of family as based on marriage and kinship we have a belief that its meaning transcends specific domestic arrangements and provides a basis for wider genealogical identification, patterns of inheritance, and the rights and obligations associated with consanguinity.

---

[4] *New English Dictionary on Historical Principles.*
[5] *Families in Former Times,* Cambridge 1979.

It is, perhaps, not surprising that a term whose connotations have so much resonance should have the symbolic significance that it does. Criticism of the family can be perceived simultaneously as criticism of both day-to-day living arrangements and of wider patterns of kinship and their meaning. The difficulty of placing any particular usage of the term family is not a merely technical or academic one. It underlies the many contradictions in analyses of household, sexuality and kinship, and is the root of the apparently inexplicable failure to develop a systematic understanding of the history of these arrangements. Confusing, as these various definitions do, the empirical analysis of household organization with ideological, political, moral and religious dimensions of sexuality and kinship, has led to serious problems of interpretation. These difficulties are not simply analytic, however, since the analyses themselves are locked in political positions related to the desirability of the various possible arrangements. The definition of 'family' is in itself a politically contested one and the vehemence with which academic and historical points of view are argued bears tribute to this fact. At present, the debate is particularly explicit about the political significance of defining specific arrangements as 'family', but these political dimensions colour discussion and interpretation at all levels. In a very precise sense 'the family' is an ideological construct and when we consider debates on 'its place in society', 'its historical development' and 'its relationship to capitalism' we have to look at the extent to which the analyses are themselves constituted in political and ideological terms. This we shall attempt to do by looking at two propositions, both the subject of continual debate but both commanding considerable popular and academic credence.

(i) 'The nuclear family is suited to the functional requirements of the capitalist mode of production.'

This proposition can be expressed in differing vocabularies; in sociology, for instance, it always used to take the form of 'a functional fit between the nuclear family and industrial society'. It is a shorthand statement that covers a number of separate arguments contrasting the family in capitalism with its supposed predecessor. The main points of the argument can be sketched out as follows:–

Capitalism needs the family to reproduce biologically the working class as labourers for capitalist production; it needs these labourers to be reproduced into the divisions of class. Whereas under feudal relations of production, the household was a unit of production and consumption, in capitalism the family is principally a unit of consumption for goods produced outside the home. Feudal society could support an extended family structure, since the majority of peasants were tied to the land, but the demand for wage labour in capitalism requires a mobile population of small families. Many features of the family in capitalism relate to this transformation. The separation of home from work led to the identification of women with childbearing and childrearing; to the development of the home as a privatized and personal realm, distinct from the public world of social production; to the assumption that women (and children) would form a secondary, or reserve, labour force rather than a primary one; to the notion that this privatized family would in the main be supported by a breadwinner's wage. Over time this family form became adept at the task of socializing children into appropriate expectations of class (and gender) and has taken on a conservative role in the transmission of capitalist ideology. The split between the public world of work and the private life at home provides an integrated mechanism for reducing the worker's alienation and compensating for the cash-nexus character of capitalist society.

This series of points, though obviously a simplified statement of some complex arguments, represents a train of thought that has achieved considerable consensus. Indeed many of the elements are regularly put forward as accepted truth, or simply assumed prior to discussion. It would be possible to analyse the points one by one and demonstrate contradictory evidence or theoretical weaknesses in them all. Such an exhaustive exercise is beyond our present scope, but we do want to take up some of the most interesting problems for discussion.

In the first place it is probably not widely appreciated that the shift from the extended to the nuclear family, so confidently mentioned in everything we read, is a phenomenon for which little decisive empirical evidence can be found. Peter Laslett maintains that the family in England prior to industrialization always was nuclear, with a mean household size of 4.75 remaining constant from the sixteenth century to the end of the nineteenth. Indeed he regards the notion of the extended family as an ideology, existing in the minds of social scientists rather than in fact, representing an uncritical reading of the ignorant sociologist Frederick Le Play and some obscure desire to evoke a 'world we have lost'.[6] On the other hand we have the equally vehemently stated findings of the classic study *Family and Kinship in East London*, whose authors found – much to their surprise – that the extended family was alive and well and living in Bethnal Green in the 1950s.[7] Young and Wilmott's findings challenged the assumption of the nuclear family by describing a community in which three-generational families were common, and links between mothers, daughters and grandchildren the central organizing principle of family life. This, however, is merely one instance of a more general pattern of the population not inhabiting the nuclear family households to which social scientists have consigned it. Questions of statistical interpretation necessarily arise here, and of the relationship between household and family. It may be, for example, that mean household size could remain constant while the meaning of 'family' and the relations between such households changed considerably.

Empirical difficulties arise with many other aspects of the classic analysis (classic, at least, in most social-scientific and Marxist thought). Is the family principally a unit of consumption? One incontrovertible outcome of the spate of work in the 1970s on the political economy of domestic labour was the

---

[6] Peter Laslett, *Household and Family in Past Time*, and *The World We Have Lost*, New York 1965.
[7] Michael Young and Peter Willmott, London 1957.

demonstration that within the home a considerable amount of *production* is carried out. So although the role of the family in maintaining high levels of consumption is important, it cannot be said that production has slipped completely out of the domestic sphere.

Does the family in a nuclear form facilitate the mobility of labour? Again, an analytic shibboleth looks rather more contradictory than we could hope. Perhaps it did at one stage, but labour mobility is now mainly associated with groups of workers who are disadvantaged and vulnerable for quite other reasons. Migrant labour (be it Irish to England in the nineteenth century or the position of European 'guest-workers' today) finds it difficult to protect even the most tiny of nuclear families from the privations and separations engendered by the employment of the wage-earner. Indeed the classic cases are those where families are split up and payments home are the order of the day for workers who may even be housed in barracks or hostels. It should be recognized, however, that it is precisely the immobility of the nuclear family-based household that creates the hyper-exploited situation of that most vulnerable of all groups of workers, the married women home-workers on very low piece-work rates.

Building on these questions, we may ask: to what extent *are* home and work separated? Recent feminist work has tended to challenge too rigid a distinction here. Leonore Davidoff, for example, points to a particular form of 'intermediate enterprise' – taking in paid lodgers – that was very common in the nineteenth century.[8] We know that in the present recession the growth of the informal economy has blurred yet further the distinction between work undertaken for cash payment and the supposedly non-cash character of the family-household. As far as gender division is concerned, there are many continuities between home and work. The character of women's paid work, as Sally Alexander and other feminists have pointed out, owes so much to tasks traditionally ascribed to women in the

---

[8] 'The Separation of Home and Work?', in S. Burman, ed., *Fit Work for Women*, London 1979.

household that it can be seen as an extension of them.[9] More recently, feminists have emphasised how gender identities are not merely transported into the workplace but are created and structured there in definitions of femininity and masculinity that in turn feed back into the domestic meaning of gender.[10] One of the most difficult and complex questions to arise from the discussion is how far we should accept the thesis 'hat capitalism and the privatization of the family are connected to each other. Eli Zaretsky and others see a distinctive shift under capitalism towards the construction, within the domestic sphere, of the realm of the personal.[11] This is taken to include a heightening of emotionality, a more significant investment in relationships, and a greater degree of introspection and self-consciousness. It could be related to developments later on towards a romantic-choice rather than an arranged concept of marriage, as Edward Shorter argues,[12] and it could also be seen as part of the more general tendency towards individualism usually identified as a feature of capitalism. It is not coincidental that the theses of Zaretsky and Shorter have, for different reasons, proved controversial. Historians of what Michael Anderson has called the 'sentiments school' find it very difficult to demonstrate their arguments convincingly. Attitudes, personality traits, consciousness are hard enough to analyse in contemporary subjects, leave alone for periods of history when we must ever be projecting our own subjectivity and conceptual categories onto the evidence.

The distinction between private and public is an important one and it is reasonable to argue that the character of production under capitalism exacerbates, if it does not actually create, a split between the domestic and social spheres. There are dangers, however, in posing this distinction itself as a determining one. The construction of 'the family' as a priv-

[9] Sally Alexander, 'Women's Work in Nineteenth-century London', Mitchell and Oakley, eds., *The Rights and Wrongs of Women.*
[10] See Cynthia Cockburn, 'The Material of Male Power', *Feminist Review*, no. 9, 1981.
[11] *Capitalism, the Family and Personal Life.*
[12] *The Making of the Modern Family*, London 1976.

atized zone with rigid barriers to prevent the intrusion of the social is an ideological process rather than a given of capitalist society. Richard Sennett observes that 'all too often in writings on the private family . . . it is assumed that privatization can accomplish its own goals, that people who desire to create little hidden regions of open emotional expression in society can actually do so . . . it is an attempt which constantly fails, precisely because the alien world organizes life within the house as much as without it'.[13] In analysing the significance – and oppressiveness – of privatization we need to ensure that we do not reproduce at the level of theory a distinction that has been constructed historically and ideologically. This distinction between public and private should be an object of analysis not a conceptual tool.

One major problem of the attempt to argue a functional relationship between a particular form of family and a particular mode of production is that we have to accept the family as it is constructed ideologically – as a self-evident unity – in order to do so. Hence we tend to idealize 'the pre-capitalist family' and project onto 'the capitalist family' all the evils of capitalism. Deconstruction of this supposed unity involves a number of processes. To begin with we need a closer analysis of arrangements of kinship, sexuality and the household as they vary culturally and by class. No description of the family will hold true across classes or in a multi-cultural society such as Britain. In this sense, recent detailed research on the family forms associated with particular class and ethnic groups is an extremely welcome development.[14]

Deconstruction of 'the family' also throws some light on what are often understood as the 'contradictory effects' of capitalism on the family. Juliet Mitchell identifies several such contradictions in her consideration of the ideology of the family: 'Thus the ideology of the family can remain: individua-

[13] 'Destructive Gemeinschaft', in Robert Boocock *et al.*, eds., *An Introduction to Sociology*, London 1980, p. 109.

[14] See the exemplary study by Mary Ryan, *Cradle of the Middle Class: The Family in Oneida County, New York, 1790–1865*, Cambridge 1981; and Verity Saifullah Khan, ed., *Minority Families in Britain*, London 1979.

lism, freedom and equality, (at home you're "yourself"), while the social and economic reality can be very much at odds with such a concept. The contradictions between the ideological intentions of the family and its socio-economic base do not mean that we say the former is false . . . The family is the most fundamental (the earliest and most primitive) form of social organization. When, under capitalism, it was made to embody as an ideal, what had been its economic function under feudalism, a chronic contradiction took place.'[15] The distinction between the economic and ideological dimensions of the family has been further elaborated by Irene Bruegel, who argues that 'capitalism both tends to destroy the family and to maintain it; and in this contradiction lies the conflicting pressures on women and working-class women particularly, which render the situation fluid and not determined.'[16]

An analysis couched in terms of contradictions is certainly more satisfactory than a complacent evocation of tidy functional relationships. We need to ask, however, whether such contradictions are generated within the dynamic of capitalist production relations or whether they are a consequence of perceiving the family as a unified category. Put another way, if 'the family' is an ideologically constructed unity imposed on changing sets of heterogeneous arrangements, it is not surprising that we find contradictions in the action of capitalism on such arrangements.

These questions all bring into play the difficulties arising from not merely a functionalist, but an extremely essentialist, conception of 'the family'. The supposed suitability of a nuclear family form to the capitalist mode of production raises problems not because *any* functionalist formulation necessarily arouses suspicion but because it takes for granted both the empirical existence of such a family form as a dominant type and because it endows it with a quite spurious unity and coherence. The objections we raise have been most summarily expressed by C.C. Harris, who writes: 'there is no "family" in

---

[15] *Woman's Estate*, Harmondsworth 1971, pp. 156–7.
[16] 'What Keeps the Family Going?', *International Socialism*, 2, 1, 1978, p. 12.

general upon which another process such as "industrialization" has effects. "Industrialization" no more deprived "the
family" of its productive economic function than the development of the family as a unit of consumption caused the spread
of "industrialization". . . . One does not have to be a Marxist,
merely historically informed and conceptually competent, to
recognize the whole debate about industrialization "decom-
posing" the extended family to be the empirical and philosophical nonsense that it is.'[17]

*(ii) 'The family has declined and much of its work is now
undertaken by the state.'*

This proposition has more immediate political purchase than
that concerning capitalism and the nuclear family, but it forms
part of the same train of thought. The family as a social
institution is seen as having a historical trajectory, developing
into a privatized nuclear form which is then vulnerable to state
intervention in matters relating to the reproduction of a
domesticated workforce. Evidence of the family being 'taken
over' by the state tends to fall in two categories. The first,
usually invoked by those who bemoan it, is the rise in divorce
and illegitimacy and the supposed decline in devotion to family
values. The second, more broadly acknowledged, being the
increased role of state provision in care of the sick, aged and
unemployed, and in the education of children.

These themes are well-trodden ground and it is not necessary
for us to review the debate in detail. Two points must be
stressed, however, in arriving at a view on it. The first is that,
without exception, analyses of the relationship between family
and state are linked to specific political positions. The second is
that the way in which the relationship is posed depends upon
what 'the family' is taken to represent. This may sound
obvious, but it is of considerable significance. We can begin to

[17] 'The Changing Relation between Family and Societal Form in Western Society',
in Michael Anderson, ed., *Sociology of the Family*, Harmondsworth 1980 (second,
revised edn.), p. 405.

consider this by looking at what David Morgan has set out as the four possible positions on a debate that involves 'an interrelated set of arguments about facts and values'.[18] Morgan says the options are:
1. The family is in decline and this is socially detrimental.
2. The family is in decline and this is either all to the good or a natural stage in the evolution of mankind.
3. The family is not in decline and this is all to the good.
4. The family is not in decline and this is socially and individually detrimental.

Morgan comments that the main debate is between 1, the position of moral entrepreneurs and thought of as the 'popular' view, and 3, the main position taken by sociologists. Options 2 and 4 are relatively marginal.

Seen in this way, the principal assumption at the heart of the 'declining family' debate is that the family is the site of moral values. What is at stake between the moral entrepreneurs and the sociologists is the definition of family morality. The classic instance of this is Ronald Fletcher's pop-sociology book, *The Family and Marriage in Britain*,[19] which argues that the contemporary family is a vast improvement on any earlier versions. Responsibilities for health and education are lifted from its shoulders, the availability of divorce has made marriage much more popular and stable, the family is now much less oppressive to women and children – in short, it provides a much nicer environment for its basic job of providing warm affective relationships in a home with a relatively high standard of living. Fletcher believes that the family is now a more satisfying, equal and fulfilling means of providing sexual relationships, parenthood and home-making. In some respects, this 'sociological' view is in harmony with the moral entrepreneurs who wish to support Christian family values and the moral authority of the family. The disagreement is about what constitutes moral value. The view of Fletcher and the many others taking up this line of thinking is that 'the

[18] D.H.J. Morgan, *Social Theory and the Family*, London 1975, pp. 88–9.
[19] Harmondsworth 1966.

family' represents warm human relationships – it is assumed to be the locus of affection and emotion. They therefore disagree with those who see the family as representing not so much affection as authority, and a code of behaviour that children should be socialized to maintain irrespective of their desires. A different view again of what the family represents can be traced to the meaning of family as household. If we take an economic rather than an affective view of the family it is much more plausible to argue that the 'functions of the family' have been usurped by the state. A crucial question here, and one of considerable political resonance, is that of economic responsibility for people not able to support themselves through wage labour. As we noted in chapter 2, the left has consistently argued that this be a responsibility of the state, and the right has consistently tried to resist these demands and to make the family responsible. If we conceptualize the family in this way, then it and the state are functional alternatives, as we recognize in the political struggles over closing of old people's homes, hospitals, or institutions for the disabled.

Among the many other possible assumptions or arguments about what the family represents are two that we discuss in detail later in this chapter. The first is the view of Christopher Lasch, who would reject outright the liberalism and complacency of the Fletcher school: 'In fact, the so-called functions of the family form an integrated system. It is inaccurate to speak of a variety of functions, some of which decline while others take on added importance. The only function of the family that matters is socialization; and when protection, work, and instruction in work have all been removed from the home, the child no longer identifies with his parents or internalizes their authority in the same way as before, if indeed he internalizes their authority at all.'[20] This, at least, is refreshingly decisive and it is a merit of Lasch's work that he poses the issues so clearly – including the evaluative ones.

---

[20] *Haven in a Heartless World*, New York 1977, p. 130.

Second, we will respond differently to the question about the family and the state if we take the view that the principal significance of the family lies in the construction of gender identity and gendered subjectivity. If we see the production of femininity and masculinity as the central work of the family, we shall be led to rather different conclusions on the relationship between these processes and the state.

Looking at this range of possible reactions to the proposition we started out with, it is clear that one can subscribe to it in quite varying ways (if at all) that will depend upon the meaning ascribed to the term family. Once again we come up against the problem that 'the family' is a constructed unity rather than a term on whose real referent or meaning we can agree. It is now widely recognized that the tendency to think in terms of an 'essential' family creates serious theoretical problems and confusions. The solution to these problems is, however, rather less clear. The approach taken in the recent work of Jacques Donzelot has been much discussed as a means of engaging with the question of family and state in such a way as to circumvent these theoretical difficulties. As the only serious candidate for this claim, his work merits some detailed consideration.

Donzelot's *The Policing of Families* first appeared in 1977 in France, and was published in Britain in 1980.[21] It is a difficult book to summarize and the text does not readily deliver an argument for objective description by a neutral reader. Any account of the book will tend to reflect the preoccupations of the reader, and ours is no exception. Donzelot's book is characterized by an explicit rejection of the humanism, moralism, subjectivism, culturalism and essentialism that haunt discussion of the family. It seeks to apply Foucault's micro-historical method and to describe what exists in the various practices in which the family is enmeshed, rather than to locate the family in a pre-given theoretical or historical framework.

---

[21] *La Police des Familles*, Paris 1977; *The Policing of Families*, New York 1979, London 1980 (translated by Robert Hurley). References are to the London edition.

The flavour of Donzelot's method, and style, can be captured from the passage in his preface to the English translation where he sets out his approach in contrast to that of the school of Ariès and Flandrin. 'The method we have employed tries to avoid this danger by positing the family, not as a point of departure, as a manifest reality, but as a moving resultant, an uncertain form whose intelligibility can only come from studying the system of relations it maintains with the socio-political level. This requires us to detect all the political mediations that exist between the two registers, to identify the lines of transformation that are situated in that space of intersections.'[22]

Donzelot's characterization of the family as a site of intersections rather than a pre-given institution is radically deconstructive. A central preoccupation of the book is the construction of the realm of 'the social' in and through the processes that are described in connection with the family. The text is 'deconstructive' in two further important senses. It rejects a unitary notion of the family and devotes considerable attention to the class differences in play, and stresses that the processes constructing bourgeois family practice are quite distinct from those relating to the working-class family. Donzelot also rejects what he sees as characteristic of a functionalist Marxist perspective – the tendency to pose the family as a retrogressive institution and to attribute to 'false consciousness' or ideology the investment so many people make in it.

Two related theses dominate *The Policing of Families*: disappearance of the family as a protagonist, and the creation of the sphere of the social. Donzelot describes a change from government *of families* to government *through the family*. He sees the family of the Ancien Régime – say in the mid eighteenth century – as continuous with public power. The head of household wielded power over his family 'precisely in so far as this power was in keeping with the requirements of public order'.[23] The *lettres de cachet de famille*, enabling the

[22] *Policing*, p. xxv.
[23] *Policing*, p. xx.

head to imprison his children for not living up to their family obligations, illustrate the way in which family authority was endorsed and supported by the state. This situation gave way, as a result of changes both within and outside the family, to one where families lost this authority. By the mid twentieth century 'the family appears as though colonized'.[24] The family of the Ancien Régime, capable of standing apart from established power, gives way to the modern family which has become 'a relay, an obligatory or voluntary support for social imperatives'.[25] As Donzelot neatly puts it: 'From being the plexus of a complex web of relations of dependence and allegiance, the family became the nexus of nerve-endings of machinery that was exterior to it'.[26]

Although Donzelot refers to these processes as a shift from family patriarchalism to a patriarchy of the state, his account of the mechanisms involved does not employ the notion of the state as an agent. He stresses instead the various interventions that occur in different settings. The richness of his account cannot be rendered here and we can merely give some examples of the themes he considers. In the nineteenth century, he argues, there develops an alliance between the medical profession and hygiene technicians and the mother of the bourgeois family. She it is who is to become the ally of the 'experts', the educator of the family and the executor of the experts' orders. Donzelot sees in this process an alliance of moralizing philanthropy and promotional feminism, working for the construction of what – in another vocabulary – might be called the ideology of domesticity. The children of the bourgeoisie, under this benevolent maternalism, grow up in 'supervised freedom'; for the working class it spelt increased *surveillance*. Donzelot argues that 'the strategy of familializing the popular strata rested on the instruction of the woman, who was given the weapon of social housing . . . and told how to use it: keep strangers out so as to bring the husband and especially the

---

[24] *Policing*, p. 103.
[25] *Policing*, p. 92.
[26] *Policing*, p. 91.

children in.'[27] In this way the independent authority of families gave way to social management through families and increased intervention and supervision of the family. This he calls the 'tutelary complex'

Donzelot goes on to pay considerable attention to the form of management developed in the twentieth century. The 'social' problems caused by inadequate families were to be resolved by a technology of expert supervision of family relations. For this purpose, the 'relational technicians' found psychoanalysis, in a diluted and modified form, the most appropriate means. Psychoanalysis succeeded as an answer to two objectives that Donzelot poses as a question: '*How could the family be divested of a part of its ancient powers – over the social destiny of its children, in particular – yet without disabling it to a point where it could not be furnished with new educative and health-promoting tasks?*'[28] From this problem arises the elaborate structure of counselling, guidance, advice, management and supervision by statutory and voluntary agencies that Donzelot describes as 'psy'. He sees the social significance of psychoanalysis as lying in its subtly disabling character: 'psychoanalysis ratifies and valorizes the conventional family arrangements, the role of the father, the role of the mother, but at the same time it reduces their former strategic disposition to a mere skeleton, serving only as a constellation of images, a surface of induction for relations, a *functional simulacrum*.'[29]

Throughout *The Policing of Families* Donzelot amplifies his main themes of the weakening of the family and the creation of the realm of the social. A key aspect of this is his understanding of familialism, and familialization. The complex character of the relation between the family and the social is made clear at the outset: 'This first object, the family, will thus be seen to fade into the background, overshadowed by another, the social, in relation to which the family is both queen and prisoner.'[30] The social is constituted, in part, from aspects of the family.

[27] *Policing*, p. 40.
[28] *Policing*, p. 199 (emphasis original).
[29] *Policing*, p. 226–7.
[30] *Policing*, p. 7.

Although the family as an organic basis for social order is undermined, Donzelot insists that 'familialism was the locomotive to which all the elements of today's policy in matters of sexuality, reproduction, and education were progressively attached.'[31] In this emphasis Donzelot is surely right. Perhaps the most significant contribution made by *The Policing of Families* is this insistence on the distinction between the family as a protagonist and the diffusion of familialism in the sphere of the social. On this one point we concur with those who have heralded Donzelot's book as a breakthrough in debates about the family. There is much to be said on the other side, however.

It is worth mentioning, in a preliminary way, the extraordinarily superior tone of this text. Our summary of the argument does less than justice to the self-conscious literary pretensions and the intellectual inflation inherent in the presentation of the book as a whole. It is inaccessible and elitist in more than its dense and idiosyncratic vocabulary and syntax. In the preface to the English edition Donzelot does briefly locate the context of the work, but as originally published in France it descends on the unwary reader with no hint as to the debate in which it is inserted. This rather olympian detachment is reflected in the pseudo-scientificity of the style — for example, the reference to 'results' of archival work, which are nothing but the subjective reading and interpretation of documents that historians normally hedge with methodological qualifications.

It is as if Donzelot seeks to lift himself out of the vulgar political mêlée on these matters and to provide an apolitical and objective knowledge about them. Here, at last, is the truly value-free account of the family. Paul Hirst sees it as a virtue that Donzelot refuses to take sides. 'He chooses not to judge the scientific or political status of psychoanalysis, but, rather, seeks to explain its practical effect'. And again, 'he does not take "sides" in the thorny question of the rights of parents

[31] *Policing*, p. 198.

versus the needs of children for care and protection. He subscribes neither to the ideology of liberal individualism nor to that of welfarism. He asks instead what relations *exist* between law, psychiatry and education, and how does social work actually operate as a crucial component of the 'tutelary complex'?[32] Who is this paragon who subscribes to no ideologies and has no views on controversial questions? As we shall show later, Donzelot has very clear political positions and the attempt to depoliticize academic knowledge and present it as objective is – as usual – mystificatory.

Another aspect of the mystification in this text can be seen in Donzelot's treatment of Marxism's failure to engage with the appeal of the family. He poses the problem very well, and it is worth quoting his assessment of the weakness of functionalist Marxism on this point: 'If today's family were simply an agent for transmitting bourgeois power, and consequently entirely under the control of the "bourgeois" state, why would individuals, and particularly those who are not members of the ruling classes, invest so much in family life? To assert that this is the result of ideological impregnation comes down to saying, in less delicate language, that these individuals are imbeciles, and amounts to a not-too-skilful masking of an interpretative weakness.'[33] Paul Hirst rightly comments that Donzelot's question challenges both Marxism and feminism, and that we cannot use the concept of ideology to explain the fact that (in the present) 'families are, like it or not, formed by acts of choice of the partners'.[34] The question is an extremely interesting one, though Hirst ignores the social pressures surrounding individual 'choices', and both Marxism and feminism need to engage seriously with it. We may legitimately ask, though, whether Donzelot himself can give any answer to it. He cannot. Having posed for himself the question why individuals have conceived an attachment to the family, the answer he comes up

---

[32] Paul Hirst, 'The Genesis of the Social', *Politics and Power*, 3, 1981, pp. 69–70, 75.
[33] *Policing*, p. 52.
[34] 'The Genesis of the Social', p. 71.

with is: *because*. More precisely, because over a period of time it came to be regarded as positive.[35] We do not seek to make a cheap point here. Donzelot raises a useful question even if he provides no satisfactory answer. The reason why his treatment of this issue (and indeed Paul Hirst's) is mystificatory is that the question raised is one which by definition Donzelot can never answer. It is, in its concern with individual affection, need and choice, a question that can arise only in a humanist perspective. No anti-humanist theoretical discourse could ever answer it, and to pose it is therefore inappropriate, even opportunist. Donzelot is not interested in the attempts of some Marxists to answer his question,[36] it is merely a stick with which to beat the others.

This leads on to a further set of related issues concerning *The Policing of Families*. The entire book, as both Donzelot and his English reviewers have remarked, is cast in a theoretical framework that rejects that version of Marxism which sees the family as functionally necessary for capitalism. Indeed it would be reasonable to suggest that this underlies the interest in and popularity of the book. But let us be clear about this: what Donzelot rejects is not functionalism (Marxist or any kind) but the agents normally constituted in Marxist analysis. *The Policing of Families* is a thoroughly functionalist text. Some examples are necessary to demonstrate this point: 'the family is an agency whose incongruity with respect to *social requirements* can be reduced, or *made functional*, through the establishment of a procedure that brings about a "floating" of social norms and family values'; 'these are the things that made

---

[35] 'The fact that the discourses denouncing social privilege and class domination had to dissociate themselves gradually from the critique of the family; that demands slowly came to be based on the defence and improvement of family living conditions of the "disadvantaged"; that the family became at the same time the point where criticism of the established order stopped and the point of support for demands for more social equality: all this is sufficient invitation to regard the family and its transformation as a positive form of solution to the problems posed by a liberal definition of the state rather than as a negative element of resistance to social change.' *Policing*, p. 53.

[36] One recent attempt to explain why the working-class has invested in the family is Jane Humphries, 'Class Struggle and the Persistence of the Working Class Family', *Cambridge Journal of Economics*, vol. 1, no. 3, 1979.

the family into the *essential figure* of our societies, into the *indispensable correlate* of parliamentary democracy'.[37] Certainly Donzelot rejects the mechanical version of the 'reproduction thesis' that the family is an agent of the reproduction of capitalist social relations. But he accepts this in a modified form by saying (a) that it was true of the Ancien Régime family and (b) that social agencies intervene at the point of the family's failures. This latter argument is extremely telling. Cited by Paul Hirst as a tribute to Donzelot's critique of Marxist functionalism, it is, in its assumption that intervention follows dysfunction in the system, a classic functionalist position.[38]

The functionalism of Donzelot's formulations is intrinsic to the way he poses all the issues and to the language he uses to describe events.[39] Indeed at times the approach is what might once have been called conspiracy theory. Of the 'alliance' between moral philanthropy and feminism he says: 'This was not a matter of discourse but of active alliances and effective operations.'[40] However, the central issue in all of this is not the question of functionalism as normally posed. Donzelot's is a functionalist text; but what is radical about his approach, and the reason why his work has been taken up from an anti-functionalist position, is that he rejects the integrated logic of a functionalist perspective. Specifically, he rejects the Marxist concepts of a capitalist state and of a bourgeois class as agents seeking to secure interests. These entities are radically deconstructed and replaced by contingent, miscellaneous and arbitrary agencies. The question of *agency* is in fact the central refusal of Donzelot's text. It is not the method of 'Marxist functionalism' that is in question at all, it is the analytic categories of Marxism whose validity is being challenged. It is

---

[37] *Policing*, pp. 8, 94 (our emphasis).

[38] Indeed one of us has been criticized for arguing it. See Diana Adlam's review, 'The Case Against Capitalist Patriarchy', *m/f*, no. 3, of Mary McIntosh's 'The State and the Oppression of Women' (Annette Kuhn and AnnMarie Wolpe, eds., *Feminism and Materialism*, London 1978).

[39] See *Policing*, pp. 8, 37, 39, 44, 73, 77, 94, 199, 220 for examples.

[40] *Policing*, p. 36.

interesting that concepts like 'Ancien Régime' and 'parliamentary democracy' – never subjected to critical analysis – take the place of the Marxist categories of state and bourgeoisie. What is curious, of course, is why the method should be retained – why the vocabulary of 'effects' is used when the concept of 'cause' is denied. The account throughout is militaristic in tone and imagery: strategy, surveillance, tactic, supervision, intervention, instrument, weapon, means, mechanism, alliance, operation. The notion of a 'non-intentional strategy', invoked by Attar Hussein and Jill Hodges in their interpretation of Donzelot[41], appears to us to be a fruitless contradiction in terms.

Donzelot's deconstruction of the state and the bourgeoisie is only partially complemented by a deconstruction of the family, despite this latter being the more obvious purpose of his book. The family is historically deconstructed in the course of his narrative – from the 'protagonist' of the Ancien Régime to the nexus of intersections that is the modern family – but it is not theoretically deconstructed. In 'the transition from a government of families to a government through the family'[42] we find evoked the original family as, we might say, a subject in history, an agent with powers, an institution with authority. Compared with Donzelot's treatment of the later, weaker, family, it is universalized. He refers back to it as 'the family' in general – even though we have been introduced to it as the family form of a particular class. It is not too fanciful to read this as residual essentialism, as an idealized evocation of 'the family' we have now lost.

Certainly there is considerable evidence to suggest that Donzelot is not the objective commentator he has been portrayed as being. Feeding as it does into the emotional rhetoric of an idealized family, the title of Donzelot's book is in itself instructive. When it comes to being *policed*, we all know whose side we are on. We have said earlier that defence of an idealized 'family' invariably carries anti-feminist implications.

[41] *Ideology and Consciousness*, no. 5.
[42] *Policing*, p. 92.

Leaving aside the contentious reading of this book by Paul Hirst, who concludes that feminism must struggle *within* rather than against, the family – and the reaction this has generated[43] – we can see this tendency in the book itself. Donzelot regards the modern family as 'pathological': 'with its saturation by hygienic, psychological, and pedagogical norms, it becomes harder to distinguish the family from the disciplinary continuum of the social apparatuses.'[44] It is, of course, relevant that Donzelot has established at an early stage the guilt of the wife – it is she who is in alliance with the doctors, collaborating with the experts and technicians. Feminism was at least partially responsible for this, and in an uncharacteristic lapse into a well-known political cliché Donzelot refers to the housewife and mother as the instrument who is to 'stamp out the spirit of independence in the working man'.[45]

Underlying *The Policing of Families* is a very familiar theme. The authoritarian patriarchal family is mourned, and women are blamed for the passing of this organic basis of social order. The text is incipiently anti-feminist, and even at times explicitly conjures up for the reader's sympathy the 'poor family' and the henpecked husband.[46] The distance between Donzelot's treatment of the 'psy' complex and a feminist perspective can be seen by comparing his consideration of the expertise of 'the social' with the approach of Barbara Ehrenreich and Deirdre English. *For Her Own Good: 150 Years of the Experts' Advice to Women* covers much the same ground as *The Policing of Families* – medical, paediatric, educational

---

[43] Fran Bennett *et al.*, 'Feminists – the Degenerates of the Social?', *Politics and Power*, 3, 1981.

[44] *Policing*, p. 227.

[45] *Policing*, p. 36.

[46] *Policing*, p. 103: 'A paradoxical result of the liberalization of the family, of the emergence of children's rights, of a re-balancing of the man-woman relationship: the more these rights are proclaimed, the more the stranglehold of a tutelary authority tightens around the poor family. In this system, family patriarchalism is destroyed only at the cost of a patriarchy of the state. The very frequent absence of the father testifies to this. Because he is busy working? Certainly, but that is not the whole of it, for when he is present, nine times out of ten it is only in order to keep quiet and let his wife do the talking.'

and psychoanalytic interventions – but women are not seen as collaborators with the enemy and nor are they blamed for the demise of the patriarchal family in all its glory.[47] As we shall argue later, Donzelot's analysis has much in common with that of Christopher Lasch, whose position in relation to feminism – confrontational though it is – is at least clearly expressed and open to debate.

2. Subjectivity and Authority

Propositions about the family's relation to the needs of industrial capitalism, or to the state, are obviously concerned with the place of the family in society generally. We want now to concentrate on debates about the internal dynamics of the family.

Social scientists have traditionally studied two main aspects of life within the family. On the one hand, the family is seen as the focus of affective life, removed from the cash-nexus of a contractual society; on the other hand, the crucial dimension of its operations is identified as 'socialization'. In the family children are socialized into appropriate roles and acculturated to appropriate status expectations. Many classic studies documented the ways in which styles of childrearing – varying by social class – accomplished this all-important task.

Feminists have tended to stress the inegalitarianism and coercion that permeate the affective side of family life. They have, however, tended to accept the importance of the socializing function, and have introduced a new aspect of it: *gender* socialization. Feminism's distinction between sex and gender, as biological and social categories respectively, paves the way for an exploration of how gender is constructed in childhood. Simone de Beauvoir's opening remarks in her chapter on 'childhood' (in *The Second Sex*) have set the scene

---

[47] London 1979. Ehrenreich and English, on the contrary, see women as broadly speaking – the victims rather than villains of the piece. This approach, too, is not without problems, but the comparison does suggest that historical interpretations of this kind are not politically neutral.

for the feminist project of analysing socialization: 'One is not born, but rather becomes, a woman. No biological, psychological or economic fate determines the figure that the human female presents in society; it is civilization as a whole that produces this creature, intermediate between male and eunuch, which is described as feminine.'[48]

Feminist analysis of gender socialization has been in many respects revelatory and consciousness-raising. A succession of powerful accounts of familial, and more general, processes involved in the construction of passive, dependent femininity have proved both educationally and politically useful. However, the concept of 'socialization' is not without problems, and it needs to be used with some caution. Its principal weakness is that it tends to assume a pre-given content that is mechanically transmitted from one generation to the next: 'roles' already exist in society, and the task of 'socialization' is to funnel people into them as actors in a play whose script is already written.

Academic social science has found the perspective whose vocabulary consists of 'sex roles', 'socialization' and 'stereotypes' much the easiest version of feminism to swallow. This perspective dominates academic women's studies in Britain, and – more strongly – in the United States. The approach could be illustrated as follows: 'Socialization is the transmission of behaviour, roles, attitudes and beliefs to the next generation. By direct prescription, by example and by implicit expectation, a variety of people in a variety of relationships influence the growing individual. Gradually the child *internalizes* what s/he has been taught . . . . Socializing agents hold stereotypical beliefs about sex-appropriate characteristics. Sex-role socialization reflects expectations based upon these beliefs.'[49] The key term here is *transmission* – of roles and beliefs already constituted before the individual acquires them.

[48] Harmondsworth 1974, p. 295.
[49] Helen Weinreich, 'Sex-role Socialization', Jane Chetwynd and Oonagh Hartnett, eds., *The Sex Role System*, London 1978.

The notion of socialization as transmission has both strengths and weaknesses. Clearly there are narrow and stereotypical 'roles' for women and men in our society, and there is now increased recognition of the damage done to individuals of both sexes in the attempts made – like making left-handed children use their right hand – to fit us into them. But to see socialization in this way is to consider every individual the passive victim of a monolithically imposed system. It prevents understanding of the positive acceptance of such identities – which is analysed so eloquently from an existentialist point of view by de Beauvoir, and also in psychoanalysis. It also obscures from us the extent to which these roles and expectations are *not* static and pre-given and prevents us analysing the changes that have occurred.

It is for these reasons that the concept of socialization must be, if not abandoned, at least complemented by a more adequate understanding of subjectivity. This in turn poses some different problems in relation to what is understood by ideology. Recent feminist work on these issues also raises questions about the adequacy of psychoanalytic theory and the relevance of the concept of patriarchy. We have here a cluster of interrelated problems, whose resolution appears not at present in sight but which raise the most fundamental issues for Marxism and for feminism. Clearly our conceptualization of the family will depend upon how we understand gendered subjectivity, what we mean by ideology, the credence we give to psychoanalytic theory, and the significance we attribute to patriarchy.

In the first instance it can of course be noted that Marxism, in common with other materialist approaches, has not addressed the question of subjectivity, beyond exploring a narrowly defined problem of class consciousness. The subjects of Marxism are collectivities rather than individuals. To say this is not necessarily to endorse the view that Marxism has a record of complete failure on these matters, for Marx's own discussions of alienation, fetishism, ideology, religion and consciousness are in many ways more insightful and suggestive than it has become fashionable to allow. Nevertheless, the absence of any sustained exploration of subjectivity is a major difficulty in any attempt to work with both feminist and Marxist categories. For feminism has attached a fundamental significance to lived experience, to consciousness, to subjectivity. All the evidence suggests that however tenacious class identity and class consciousness may be, they are less fundamental than gender identity and the feminine and masculine subjectivities so profoundly engrained in our personalities. To 'pass' as a member of another class, though difficult in a society like Britain, is nonetheless easier than 'passing' across the boundary of sex. Gender identity is so strong that children whose sex is wrongly assigned at birth may be operated upon as an easier way of resolving the discrepancy than an attempt to change the psychic identity of the child. We are not altogether surprised, on reading the memoir of Herculine Barbin, to find suicide the only negotiable route for a woman whose sex was reassigned to that of a man in late adolescence.[50] Stability in gender identity is certainly far more essential than stability in sexual relations or preference.

The theorization of subjectivity is, of course, the theorization of a historically specific phenomenon. A concern with subjectivity tends to be a feature of bourgeois society and goes hand in hand with the individualism in which our culture is saturated. Gender difference appears, however, to mark even this most basic orientation. For the individualism of which we speak is par excellence masculine. Simone de Beauvoir insists that it is man who is subject, transcending, and woman who is defined in relation to man – as other, as contingent, as the *second* sex, not complementary to man because she is an object, not an equal subject. De Beauvoir's emphasis on the otherness ('alterity') of women is echoed in the Lacanian view of female subjectivity as defined by *lack* of the phallus and a *negative* entry into culture. The difference between the two approaches is that while de Beavoir argues that these questions are moral ones – that women's independence and authenticity are a matter, ultimately, of values – for Lacan, the patriarchal order

---

[50] *Herculine Barbin: Memoirs*, introduced by Michel Foucault, New York 1980.

is a universal of human society, not amenable to this type of conscious, political choice. The dominant themes of accounts of female subjectivity are passivity, dependence, submission and deference. Recent feminist work on psychoanalysis, drawing on the tradition of Freud and Lacan, seeks to explore the construction of gendered subjectivity in terms of the law of the father. A glimpse of these preoccupations can be seen in Simone de Beauvoir's account of a particular stage in the development of a little girl's subjectivity. 'The relative rank, the hierarchy, of the sexes is first brought to her attention in family life; little by little she realizes that if the father's authority is not that which is most often felt in daily affairs, it is actually supreme; it only takes on more dignity from not being degraded to daily use; and even if it is in fact the mother who rules as mistress of the household, she is commonly clever enough to see to it that the father's wishes come first; in important matters the mother demands, rewards, and punishes in his name and through his authority. The life of the father has a mysterious prestige: the hours he spends at home, the room where he works, the objects he has around him, his pursuits, his hobbies, have a sacred character. He supports the family, and he is the responsible head of the family. As a rule his work takes him outside, and so it is through him that the family communicates with the rest of the world: he incarnates that immense, difficult and marvellous world of adventure; he personifies transcendence, he is God. This is what the child feels physically in the powerful arms that lift her up, in the strength of his frame against which she nestles. Through him the mother is dethroned as once was Isis by Ra, and the Earth by the Sun.'[51]

This passage is a marvellously distilled perception of the girl's subjectivity. It evokes the familial authority of the father and the material relations between husband and wife on which this is built, but it also speaks eloquently to the child's desires and needs. She is protected and reassured in the present, but in

[51] *The Second Sex*, p. 314.

this act of worship she mortgages her future independence and authenticity. De Beauvoir's account draws loosely on the spirit of Freud in this rendering of the subjective experience of family relations and the psychic patterns of father-daughter relationships. The crucial question for feminists is whether the gendered subjectivity of today really does follow the model of patriarchal authority evoked here and elaborated in contemporary uses of psychoanalysis. Juliet Mitchell's account of 'the making of a lady' provides the best-known claim for psychoanalysis as the key to understanding how femininity and masculinity are acquired.[52] Mitchell argues that psychoanalysis gives the most accurate description of (*not* prescription for) patriarchal society and that we dismiss it on pain of ignorance. We want to explore this question from a somewhat different angle, by looking at the work of the American cultural critic Christopher Lasch who, from a position sympathetic to psychoanalysis, argues that the family form it describes has now been superseded. His work has elicited considerable feminist criticism and provides a useful basis from which to assess this controversy.

Writing in *New Left Review*, Lasch restates and defends against his feminist critics the theses of his two major works, *Haven in a Heartless World: The Family Besieged* and *The Culture of Narcissism: American Life in an Age of Diminishing Expectations*.[53] Lasch believes that the 'old', 'new' and feminist left are united in clinging to a critique of the patriarchal family. Since he believes this family form to have been 'coming apart' for the last century or more, he not surprisingly regards the critique of it as both irrelevant and misleading. Lasch's position has provoked irritation and anger among feminists in the United States, as has the sympathy with which it has been received by many (male) sections of the American left. This situation is complicated by the fact that Lasch enjoys the unusual status of being a socialist with a high media profile and

[52] *Psychoanalysis and Feminism*, Harmondsworth 1974.
[53] New York 1977; New York 1979; NLR 129.

book sales in the category of national best-sellers. In Britain, however, his work is less well known, though increasingly influential in some sections of the left, and in order to engage with the political implications of his recent 'reply' to feminism it is necessary to retrace the main points of his earlier works.

Haven in a Heartless World tells the well-known story that begins, 'Once upon a time there was a real family. . .' and, describing the forces of evil that have invaded this citadel, ends with a gloomy depiction of misery for all. The narrator is a Marxist: 'The history of modern society, from one point of view, is the assertion of social control over activities once left to individuals or their families. During the first stage of the industrial revolution, capitalists took production out of the household and collectivized it, under their own supervision, in the factory. Then they proceeded to appropriate the workers' skills and technical knowledge, by means of "scientific management", and to bring these skills together under managerial direction. Finally they extended their control over the worker's private life as well, as doctors, psychiatrists, teachers, child guidance experts, officers of the juvenile courts, and other specialists began to supervise child-rearing, formerly the business of the family.'[54]

Lasch sees the family as the last stronghold of the realm of the private, now invaded by public policy and increasing state manipulation. Family relations, lived in an ethos of consumerism, are now indistinguishable from the social relations of the factory and market-place. Parental authority is replaced by a definition of parenthood as merely the obligation – by implication, the father's – to provide financial resources for the commodities desired by acquisitive and individualistic housewives and children. Lasch sees advertising and consumerism as a key aspect of the 'socialization of reproduction' – 'Like the helping professions, it undermined puritanical morality and patriarchal authority, subtly allying itself with women against

---

[54] *Haven*, pp. xiv-xv.

men, children against parents.'[55] Relations within the family
now serve only self-interest, and are combative and mercenary.
Allied to this is a devaluation of romantic love, a distaste for
passion, and the reduction of marriage to one of a series of
'non-binding commitments'.
Lasch describes these developments in ironic, indeed bitter,
terms. He regards the present family, with its Dr Spock–
dependent mother, anti-disciplinarian father, and children
who never face the rigours of Oedipal rivalry, as both a psychic
and social disaster. The family, he argues, is principally an
agent for socializing the young – indeed none of its supposed
'functions' can be separated from this goal. Socialization takes
place through the internalization of parental authority and
values, the father providing the bedrock for the conflict that
must necessarily precede the development of individual conscience, and the mother's love offering a glimpse of values that
transcend this present harshness. The family, in this process of
socializing the individual into acceptance of social values, thus
mediates between the individual and society, between instinct
and culture. Lasch regards 'the irreconcilable antagonism
between culture and instinct' as the most important insight of
Freudian psychoanalysis. 'Without this insight', he argues, 'it
becomes impossible to understand how the family mediates
between the two or to understand what happens, psychologically, when the socialization of reproduction weakens or
abolishes this mediation.'[56]
What now happens, 'psychologically', is that the conflict
played out in the paradigmatic Freudian family is indefinitely
deferred. The Oedipal crisis is the foundation for the development of responsible adulthood, Lasch insists, and the evasion
of it made possible by the decline of parental authority leads to
an infantile and narcissistic personality structure. (As we shall
see later, this is predicated upon the *boy's* rivalry with his father
and implies that the increase in narcissism is equivalent to a
general feminization of the personality.) Lasch maintains that

[55] *Haven*, p. 19.
[56] *Haven*, p. 77.

the processes described by Freud – socialization through rivalry and guilt – were actually losing power at the moment Freud brought them to light. They were characteristic of a bourgeois patriarchal family form already losing ground. Evasion of generational conflict, however, is not the same as resolution of it, and Lasch argues that it lingers on in a more primitive form. The child whose father is absent, or refuses to exert his authority, will never overcome fantasies of punishment and fears of retribution but will simply project these onto an unspecified future. 'Deferred retribution represents the price paid for undeferred gratification.'[57]

This fear of deferred retribution is projected onto the social world beyond the immediate family. Today's narcissists have an attitude of sullen resentment and resignation in the face of increasingly invasive social policies and an increasingly totalitarian state. Lasch conceives of the family as a mediator – indeed a buffer – between the individual and society, and as it is weakened so we lose the restraint but also the idealism it engendered. We become vulnerable to new forms of domination – those of consumerism and the state.

These themes are elaborated in Lasch's later, more popular, book *The Culture of Narcissism*. Children grow up unpunished by their parents and project their fears and fantasies of paternal retribution onto the arbitrary violence of a bureaucratized society. Agencies of social control adopt a permissive and therapeutic rhetoric that effectively disables authentic judgement and moral authority. Such a culture celebrates media figures and encourages narcissism and infantilism in everyone. The weakening of familial authority erodes the distinction between public and private and exposes all to 'enlightened' expert guidance on personal relations. Permissiveness, therapy and feminism all represent examples of a 'flight from feeling' – an evasion rather than an engagement with the demands of sexual relationships. These tendencies Lasch regards as both deleterious and final: 'It is too late, however, to call for a revival of the patriarchal family or even of the "companionate" family

[57] *Haven*, p. 189.

that replaced it. The "transfer of functions", as it is known in the antiseptic jargon of the social sciences – in reality, the deterioration of child-care – has been at work for a long time, and many of its consequences appear to be irreversible.'[58]

Lasch's description of the bourgeois patriarchal family is elegiac in tone, and his evident regret at the passing of this authoritarian institution has proved unpalatable to many. It is perhaps not surprising that feminists should react adversely to a writer who uses the adjective 'patriarchal' to convey approval rather than criticism. What is surprising is that despite its blatant anti-feminism, Lasch's position should have secured the credence it has on the left. This in itself belies his insistence that feminism and the left are united in a mindless attack on the family, and indeed it points to a major source of conflict between many feminists and socialists. Before considering the feminist critique of Lasch's work, however, we want to raise some rather different points for discussion.

As we are going to disagree with Christopher Lasch's history, analysis, politics and morality, we should perhaps point to some areas where we find his ideas provocative in the positive sense. Undoubtedly he is right in his identification of the real material and emotional issues so often ignored in academic work as well as in political rhetoric about the family and human relationships. We share the humanism, if you like, of his concern for real needs, and we share his insistence that the sphere of personal and psychic relations is of crucial importance for socialists. While we disagree with his answers we endorse the question that is his starting-point: 'Most studies of the family tell us everything except the things we most want to know. Why has family life become so painful, marriage so fragile, relations between parents and children so full of hostility and recrimination?'[59] In his exploration of this issue Lasch brilliantly exposes the idiocy and hypocrisy of much contemporary thinking. He subjects the oxymoronic notion of a 'non-binding commitment' to the derision it fully deserves.

[58] *Narcissism*, p. 290.
[59] *Haven*, p. xvi.

It needs to be said also that Lasch's discussion of consumerism in relation to the family provides a welcome emphasis on a strangely neglected dimension of family-household organization and familial ideology. Although the notion of the modern family as a 'unit of consumption' has been a staple truism in sociology, it has been somewhat displaced in more recent, politicized, debates on household production. Lasch writes very interestingly about advertising, the fabrication of leisure, and the mercenary and acquisitive dimensions of family relations. He presents a refreshingly crisp class analysis of the beneficiaries of what he considers the degeneration of family and individual integrity: 'Most of us can see the system but not the class that administers it and monopolizes the wealth it creates. We resist a class analysis of modern society as a "conspiracy theory". Thus we prevent ourselves from understanding how our current difficulties arose, why they persist, or how they might be solved.'[60] Although Lasch tends to present consumerism as an imposition *on* the family by the corporate state – whereas we would see familialism as a central component of consumerism – we strongly endorse his emphasis on this question.

Lasch's conception of the history of the family is, however, extremely tendentious. Quite independently of any evaluation of the psychic and social status of the family form mourned by Lasch, we can raise questions about 'the family besieged' that he invokes. In the first place, Lasch's conception of '*the* family' is quite explicitly the bourgeois model of the family characteristic of nineteenth-century capitalism – one of a variety of family forms, and quite distinct from those of the aristocracy, the proletariat and the peasantry.[61] Although Lasch emphasizes the precarious existence of this bourgeois family form, he nonetheless tends to fall back on it as an ideal-type or plumbline against which all else is measured. In the absence of rigorous periodization – let alone class and cultural specification – this type of family tends to take on a universalist and

[60] *Narcissism*, p. 376.
[61] See Mark Poster, *Critical Theory of the Family*, London 1978.

essentialist character in his accounts. As works of cultural history, these books are surprisingly vague and lacking in details of time and place. Lasch is keen to pinpoint the moment at which the family lost its force – in order to show us how it eluded the grip of psychoanalysis and the Frankfurt School by disappearing just as they pinned it down.[62] But he is less keen to document it in the moment of its prime or to show when it arose and how long it lasted. This family appears in Lasch, as does the family of the Ancien Régime in Donzelot, as a representation of what went before – a representation that seduces us into the mythology of the 'real' family.

Lasch hypostatizes the family (prior to its degeneration in the culture of narcissism) as the haven of affectivity where cash relations do not enter. It is the last thing that capitalism got hold of, conjured up with all the emotions usually reserved for the expression of horror at some programme of socialist nationalization. ('They'll be wanting to nationalize sex next'.) 'The spirit of economic rationality', writes Lasch, 'had become so pervasive in modern society that it invaded even the family, the last stronghold of pre-capitalist modes of thought and feeling.'[63]

In what sense the family is a stronghold of pre-capitalist though and feeling is never explained, and indeed it would be difficult to do so. This kind of trite assumption recurs frequently in Lasch's work, never explained and never defended. Inevitably, some of his assumptions universalize culturally specific phenomena. The idea of passionate romantic love is referred to in passing on several occasions as 'transcendent' but this claim is never substantiated. Indeed it is characteristic of Lasch that his desiderata in sexual relations emerge only from the *tone* of his account of people with whom he disagrees. Monogamy, for example, would not be explicitly

---

[62] 'Reich, Fromm, and the Frankfurt School analysed the authoritarian family at the moment of its demise. They showed how the family instils the "capacity for suffering" – for experiencing injustice as religious guilt – at the historical moment when guilt, as a means of social control, became obsolete.' *Haven*, p. 90–1. See also *Haven*, p. 180.

[63] *Haven*, p. 36.

recommended, but a critique of monogamy will be described in such a way as to make it sound silly.[64] Although Lasch is in some respects explicit about his values, he implies rather than argues the most conservative of his positions. These emerge in his treatment of family-state relations. A substantial element of his thesis is that the family has been taken over by the mushrooming guidance agencies of the corporate state. His lengthy accounts of this process are remarkably consonant with those outlined in *The Policing of Families*, and it comes as no surprise to see that the American edition of Donzelot's book carries an adulatory jacket-blurb by him. The two authors concur in diagnosing an unhealthy alliance between women and the plethora of agencies that disguise state intervention in the family as 'expertise'. In a typical passage of covert support for authoritarianism, Lasch writes: 'Enlightened opinion now identified itself with the medicalization of society: the substitution of medical and psychiatric authority for the authority of parents, priests and lawgivers, now condemned as representatives of discredited authoritarian modes of discipline.'[65]

Both Lasch and Donzelot express considerable concern at the medicalization of crime and the pervasiveness of 'therapeutic justice'. These developments, exemplified in the case of the juvenile court where the defendant is judged by probation officers, psychiatric social workers and paternalistic magistrates, tend to strip the prisoner of traditional rights in the process of removing responsibility for crime. Lasch complains that courts can then pry into family affairs, remove children from 'unsuitable' homes, and invade homes to supervise probation. Donzelot, too, waxes indignant about the abrogation of the rights of the accused in the therapeutic model of juvenile justice.[66] There is, of course, genuine cause for concern

[64] *Haven*, p. 147: 'Joining Mead, Fromm, and other celebrants of "community" he (Philip Slater) proposes to substitute a diffuse, easygoing, non-demanding warmth for the passion that fastens neurotically on a single individual, "looks backwards, hence its preoccupation with themes of nostalgia and loss", and is "fundamentally incestuous".'
[65] *Haven*, p. 100.
[66] *Policing*, p. 106–7.

in, for example, the control of prisoners with drugs and the various other abuses of the system with which we are familiar. But these are not the real causes of Lasch's (and Donzelot's) dissent: their objection is to the fact that the juvenile justice system has usurped the authority of the family, by which they mean the authority of a *father* over his children. It is the abrogation of the rights of the father, not those of the child, that draws forth their critique of juvenile courts.[67]

The question of justice is a significant one, since it symbolizes the allocation of authority. Lasch and Donzelot both imply that therapeutic justice is to be compared unfavourably with the system of confrontation between accuser and accused. Neither acknowledges the brutality and injustices of this system, which is simply invoked as more authentic, treating individuals as responsible for their actions. This position is an odd one for socialists. Forms of social justice are surely superior to the system of individual confrontation, largely based on notions of property and contract, characteristic of bourgeois democracy. If 'therapeutic justice' is to be criticized it should be with reference to systems of genuinely social control such as have existed in the past or to ideals of popular democratic justice.

Critiques of the state, and of state 'intervention' in the family, can be made from various points of view. The position taken by Lasch adopts the point of view of individualism – expressed through the notion of the authority of the father in the family. This is not as progressive as an anarchist critique of the state, let alone a socialist commitment to collective decision-making and control. It is, of course, important to recognize that Lasch's arguments apply specifically to the socialization of children under capitalism. He rightly sees the capitalist state, and the agencies and ideologies of welfarism within it, as motivated by the need to secure social control as well as promote consumerism. Yet he ignores an important

---

[67] Eli Zaretsky, taking a sharply different approach, comments that the juvenile courts tended to *protect* rather than replace the private family. 'The Place of the Family in the Origins of the Welfare State', Barrie Thorne and Marilyn Yalom, eds., *Rethinking the Family*, p. 213.

contradiction in the constitution of the welfare state: that it also represents an achievement of working-class struggle and a degree of collectivization of care. As Eli Zaretsky has pointed out, 'Lasch portrays the welfare state as the creation of middle-class reformers and professionals, ignoring the active initiative of the urban working-class and the poor in bringing about reforms'.[68] Obviously socialists can only see the social provisions of the welfare state, be it in Britain or – even more so – in the USA, as an extremely pale and inferior version of what we would wish to see in socialism. But one lesson we have learnt from the present era of savage cuts – often referred to in Britain as the 'dismantling' of the welfare state – is that the social provision of facilities (however inadequate) must be defended against the attempt to push back into the family (more accurately, onto women) the care of those who cannot care for themselves.

Lasch's approach is very different from a socialist position emphasizing struggle for improvement and democracy in social provision. It is as if his hostility to the present forms of social provision and collective responsibility for children leads him to say that the social is *necessarily* invasive and totalitarian. He repeatedly associates these elements, always contrasting them unfavourably with the familial and the individual. As socialists we would want to argue for increased social responsibility for the care and socialization of children, but to Lasch it is a matter for regret that these functions have slipped from the grip of the individualist family.

Lasch's romantic view of the psychological strengths derived from Oedipal conflict underlies his general support for authoritarian styles of socialization. This becomes evident in his fascinating discussion of the legal action taken by the state of Wisconsin in the attempt to remove children from the religious restrictions of Amish society by having them compulsorily educated in state schools. Lasch describes as sentimental liberal humanitarianism the argument made by the dissenting

<hr />

[68] Zaretsky also comments on the degree to which some feminists, seeing the welfare state as a creation of men, have ignored the role of feminists in its origins ('The Place of the Family', pp. 191–2).

judge Douglas against the right of Amish parents to control over their own children: 'The argument is sentimental above all in its assumption that the state can spare the child who does decide to break from his parents' traditions the pain, suffering, and guilt that such a break necessarily exacts – the confrontation with which, however, constitutes the psychological and educative value of such an experience. In true paternalistic fashion Douglas would smooth away the painful obstacles to the child's progress, forgetting that progress consists precisely in overcoming these obstacles.'[69]

The implications of this point of view should be noted, though they are never developed by Lasch. It is no coincidence that the suffering and guilt extolled here as conducive to the development of psychic strength – conceptualized as the equivalent of moral fibre – are the product of narrow and archaic religious dogma. Are we not being asked to believe that the crippling guilt induced by socialization through the doctrines of Roman Catholicism (for example as described by James Joyce in *A Portrait of the Artist as a Young Man*) leads to advantages denied those exposed merely to nominal Anglicanism? That the powerful residues of guilt in those who have broken from an orthodox Jewish upbringing strengthen rather than deform? Without ever defending the merits of any particular religious beliefs, Lasch tends to side with the religious against the secular. A typical example of the insertion of covert pro-religious views occurs in Lasch's discussion of the psychoanalyst Janine Chasseguet-Smirgel. Since Lasch's main thrust in this passage is to demonstrate (in a patronizing way) how her work has been misunderstood by feminists claiming to appropriate it, the reader may be forgiven for engaging with the main argument rather than with the remarks slipped in on the question of religion. Lasch suggests that, 'incidentally', Chasseguet-Smirgel may help to explain 'why the death of God has not made men more self-reliant and autonomous. On the contrary, the collapse of religious illusions has only prepared the way for more insidious illusions; and science itself, instead

[69] *Narcissism*, p. 382.

of serving as an agency of general enlightenment, helps to reactivate infantile appetites and the infantile need for illusions by impressing itself on people's lives as a never-ending series of technological miracles, wonder-working drugs and cures, and electronic conveniences that obviate the need for human effort.'[70] It could well be argued that belief in God comes fairly high on the scale of 'insidious illusions', and certainly it is responsible for more suffering in the world's history than optimism, however 'infantile', about the capacities of science. It might be 'infantile', if one were suffering from an incurable disease, to hope for the discovery of a 'wonder-drug' to cure it, but such a hope would be considerably more rational than the illusion that God would be much help.

Although we do not imply that Lasch is 'guilty by association' with religion, we feel it is relevant to observe the range and variety of conservative themes that he appears to endorse. His arguments are presented, and received, as iconoclastic *within* a socialist tradition that he characterizes as dogmatically opposed to the family. At the end of *The Culture of Narcissism* he calls, in a rare moment of optimism of the will, for the creation by citizens of 'communities of competence' and refers to 'traditions of localism, self-help, and community action that only need the vision of a new society, a decent society, to give them new vigour'.[71] The call, however, is too little and too late. His whole analysis of family and state rests on a reactionary defence of the bourgeois, patriarchal, Christian form of the family, which leads to a distorted and exaggerated account of historical change. Furthermore it is an analysis so shot through with individualism that the 'vision' of a new society so unconvincingly evoked at the last moment can inspire little confidence.

If there is doubt as to the purchase of Lasch's work on the socialist tradition, there can be little confusion about its combative stance in relation to feminism. An obvious indi-

[70] *New Left Review*, 129 (September-October 1981), p. 32.
[71] *Narcissism*, pp. 396 7.

cation of the conflict can be seen in Lasch's total silence about the oppression of women in the patriarchal family he so admires. The work of the Frankfurt School, to which Lasch is selectively indebted, provides a welcome contrast on this point: 'In the crisis of the family the latter is now presented with the reckoning, not only for the brutal oppression which the weaker women and, still more, the children frequently had to suffer at the hands of the head of the family during the initial phases of the new age, but also for the economic injustice in the exploitation of domestic labour within a society which in all other respects obeyed the laws of the market.'[72]

Lasch himself identifies feminism – along with sexual separatism, drug-taking, suicide, celibacy, promiscuity, the cult of 'cool sex' and the rise in single-person households – as part of today's 'flight from feeling'. The culture of narcissism and dependence on 'experts' have led to an increased inability to confront sexual tension and antagonism. Lasch seems to suggest that what he calls 'the routine depreciation of the opposite sex' is the best we can hope for: 'Feminism and the ideology of intimacy have discredited the sexual stereotypes which kept women in their place but which also made it possible to acknowledge sexual antagonism without raising it to the level of all-out warfare.'[73] His goal is that we should 'live more gracefully' with sexual antagonism rather than raise the stakes of the conflict or slide into passionless androgyny.

Of course, it is more difficult to be 'graceful' about antagonism when one is on the receiving end of a power structure. The principal point of conflict between Lasch and feminism is that although he appears to be treating gender relations in an objective way his standpoint is utterly and exclusively masculine. It seems extraordinary that someone whose focus is so centrally on gender should so repeatedly speak of 'children' when he is really referring only to boys. This can be seen in his

[72] 'The Family'. *Aspects of Sociology*, London 1974. p. 137. For a feminist critique of Lasch's failure to make this point see Wini Breines, Margaret Cerullo and Judith Stacey, 'Social Biology, Family Studies and Anti-Feminist Backlash', *Feminist Studies*, 4, 1978.
[73] *Narcissism*, pp. 331-2.

more sociological discussions, such as where he talks of the family pattern of the propertied classes, and in his psychoanalytic interpretations.[74] Oedipal socialization and rivalry with the father are central to Lasch's analysis, yet he fails to engage with the crucial question of the extent to which this model illuminates the psycho-sexual development of girls. Freud's discussions of female sexuality and psyche are often regarded as less satisfactory than his account of masculinity, and indeed he commented himself upon the problem. Those who accept many dimensions of Freud's approach may find his account of female sexuality less resonant or convincing. A major claim for psychoanalysis is, obviously, that it privileges questions of gender to a degree and in a manner very rarely found. At the very least, then, a challenge to Freud's account of femininity is no mere local dispute: it must be a challenge to the entire corpus. Yet Lasch treats this challenge merely as a vehicle through which the 'cultural' attack on Freud can conveniently be made. Lumping together those who sought to explore the psychology of women – from Karen Horney onwards – with those who argued as anthropologists for a cultural rather than a biological reading of Oedipal socialization, Lasch creates a category of 'revisionists'. Of course no one would disagree that the culture/instinct argument is profoundly important in psychoanalysis. But for Lasch to use this as a means for the complete marginalization of the feminist challenge simply demonstrates his fundamental unwillingness to take the question seriously.[75] No doubt he is to be congratulated for mentioning it at all.

It is interesting to note, therefore, that Lasch's defence of his theses does not actually *engage* with the arguments of his feminist critics. Stephanie Engel, in the most cogent direct response to his work, observes that, 'in a muffled form, the sense of narcissism as emasculation underlies Lasch's despair

[74] *Narcissism*, pp. 371–2; *Haven* 181–2.

[75] 'It is easy to see why the psychology of women became an issue seemingly made to order for the purpose of a "cultural" refutation of Freud. . . . Much more is at stake in this dispute than the psychology of women', *Haven*, p. 76.

over the decline of the reign of Oedipus and the emergence of narcissistic man'.[76] Engel traces this sense back to the history of Freud's distinction between anaclitic object-choice (love for someone different from oneself) and narcissistic love for an object resembling oneself. She sees the marginality of women in psychoanalytic theory as a consequence of the fact that for girls as well as boys the mother is the primary and formative object-choice: 'That women must choose to love an individual of the opposite sex when their primary love relationship would prepare them only for narcissistic object relations was a problem Freud never resolved. . . . traits such as dependence, immaturity, rigidity, and masochism have been conflated under the analytic umbrella of "narcissism", the psychological trademark of femininity.'[77] Engel argues that Lasch borrows the more pejorative of Freud's connotations of narcissism and, combining them with an idealization of the bourgeois family, arrives at a stance that systematically devalues women's experience as well as feelings of attachment, mutality, identification and relatedness.

Lasch responds to this by offering to call the culture of narcissism the culture of the uninhibited ego-ideal. For the greater part however, rather than reply to the criticism, he restates his original thesis. Patriarchy, the family and the father are a 'pseudo-problem' that merely divert the attention of the left from the real problem of the corporation and the state. Feminists are wasting their energy in a struggle against an already toppled patriarch, and meanwhile the despotism of industrial consumerism reigns unchecked.

Whatever the disagreements between Lasch and a critic such as Engel, there emerges some consensus on the point that the processes of socialization through patriarchal authority – as described by Freud – are not eternal. Lasch's account of the patriarchal family does, precisely, offer a prescription for socialization rather than a description of the current position.

[76] 'Femininity as Tragedy', *Socialist Review*, no. 53, 1980, p. 88.
[77] 'Femininity', pp. 87 8.

A recognition of the relative vulnerability and mortality of patriarchal power underlies the increased interest in recent years, in both feminist and socialist thought, of relations between women and the exploration in particular of mother-daughter relationships.

Nancy Chodorow, Dorothy Dinnerstein and Jessica Benjamin have, in different ways, contributed to this approach.[78] Although we do not wish here to examine their arguments in detail it is important to note their significance. One way of describing this would be to say that they point to the usefulness of a version of psychoanalysis that does not unduly emphasize and valorize Oedipal conflict. The internalization of the father's authority at the Oedipal moment is the basis of the boy's placement in a patriarchal order, and the weakness of the configuration for girls is the source of women's lesser inner-direction, responsibility and guilt. But to emphasize the consequences, for both sexes, of Oedipal struggle is to pay less attention to pre-Oedipal relationships. In particular, it leads to an emphasis on the patriarchal authority of the father at the expense of proper consideration of the primary relationship between a child and its mother.

This primary relationship, though not without conflict, is characterized by nurturance and attachment. So, it is argued, the later object-choices cannot be so decisive for the girl as for the boy: he can replicate the primary relation with the mother in adult heterosexuality whereas she is likely to remain at a fundamental level more torn between (heterosexual) object-choice and an attachment to relations that reproduce the intimacy and nuturance of the early bond with the mother. An approach of this kind is very different from the classic Freudian tradition. It shares many basic points, but sees Freud's stress on patriarchal authority and Oedipal socialization as the product of a particular family form in a specific period of

---

[78] Chodorow and Dinnerstein, although frequently referred to together, show marked differences of approach. See Nancy Chodorow and Susan Contratto, 'The Fantasy of the Perfect Mother', in *Rethinking the Family*, p. 72, n. 13.

history, bounded by class and culture.[79] It emphasizes the positive value we should attach to early mutuality and union and tends to downplay the significance – descriptively in the present and normatively in the future – of paternal authority. To stress the formative character of the mother-child relationship enables a revalorization of less competitive and more nurturant relationships in general and, in particular, helps to explain the history and continuance of close relations between women in later life.

In this sense, the approach developed by Nancy Chodorow and others represents both an analysis, or explanation, of the strengths of relationships – not necessarily sexual, but emotionally significant – between women, and also an insistence that their values and psychic content should be asserted against those deriving from patriarchal Oedipal socialization. Christopher Lasch considers that the project of the 'new psychoanalytic feminism' is 'the effort to uphold narcissism as a theoretical alternative to possessive individualism'.[80] More accurately, we can say that primary narcissism is to some extent rehabilitated and given a positive rather than an exclusively negative inflection.[81]

The focus of this particular approach is to argue, within a general psychoanalytic perspective, for the revaluation of 'mothering'. Jessica Benjamin argues that the feminist revolt springs from an identification with others rather than from the aggression generated by patriarchal socialization. 'It is this image of revolt springing from mutual recognition and nurtur-

[79] It is paradoxical, though welcome, that feminists have paid more attention than some others to the class boundaries of psychoanalytic theory. See Jessica Benjamin, 'Authority and the Family Revisited', *New German Critique*, no. 13, 1978, pp. 52–3.

[80] NLR, 129, p. 31.

[81] Engel makes it clear that she seeks a reconciliation rather than the one-sided position Lasch attributes to feminism. 'If one validates the autonomy of the two agencies of morality, the super-ego and the ego-ideal, not subsuming one under the other, one need not choose between the poles of terror and infinite regression. The super-ego, heir to the Oedipus complex, insists on reality and the separation of the child from the mother, whereas the ego-ideal, heir to the state of primary narcissism, restores the promise of the imagination, of desire, and the fantasy of re-fusion.' ('Femininity as Tragedy', p. 101).

ant activity which may guide us in our struggle against instrumental rationality toward a society without the father.'[82] Nancy Chodorow concludes that we also seek a world without the mother: 'Any strategy for change whose goal includes a liberation from the constraints of an unequal social organization of gender must take account of the need for a fundamental reorganization of parenting, so that primary parenting is shared between men and women.'[83] Chodorow's discussion of mothering recognizes the possibility – in her view the desirability – that mothering need not be exclusively associated with women. She describes the psychic dynamic by which socialization leads to women mothering, but argues that the generational cycle can and should be broken as men share the role of 'mother'. This raises, of course, the controversial question of whether the psychic content of mothering rests on a cultural or a biological base. Chodorow's insistence – to put it crudely – that men could 'mother' is bound to encounter the obvious rejoinder that this will be limited by the biological determination of the mother-child relationship. This stance is usually thought of as classically reactionary, whether expressed from a feminist or an anti-feminist point of view. The debate about biology, so much a feature of psychoanalytic accounts focusing on penis envy and the formation of femininity, must recur here, the question now being whether mothering is 'natural', in relation to lactation and the breast, or 'social'.

In this context, Michael Rustin has introduced an interesting discussion of Melanie Klein's work. He poses, and answers, the apposite question as to why feminists have paid so much less attention to Klein than to Freud. Klein's work does, after all 'reverse the patriarchalism' in Freud to a striking degree. Rustin stresses that Kleinianism, with its emphasis on the destructive as well as the nurturant aspects of the mother-child relation, is scarcely a sentimental account of motherhood such as might be expected to irritate feminists. 'But for all these

[82] 'Authority', p. 57.
[83] *The Reproduction of Mothering*, California 1978, p. 215.

rigorous qualities, Kleinian theory is nevertheless valorizing the caring functions predominantly assigned to women in their normal existing roles in this society. The women's movement, to put the matter rather starkly, has been chiefly seeking means to *escape* from the ideological and practical dominance of this role, into the relative freedom and apparent power which it perceives in assigned masculine functions. It has not been looking for a theoretical endorsement of the role of caring for babies.'[84]

There is a certain tension in Rustin's discussion of Klein, not unlike that found in Mitchell's account of Freud, on the question of biology. Kleinianism asserts the primacy of the social over the individual, *yet* it privileges biological parenthood. It sees femininity and masculinity as present in both sexes, *yet* it differentiates forcefully between them. It acknowledges the 'mother figure' and the bottle that substitutes for the breast, *yet* these substitutions are uneasy and unconvincing in tone. Rustin's conclusions are sensitive to the political implications of the argument – particularly in relation to feminism – but he draws the conclusion that the family will be difficult to replace if children are to be raised in a secure and stable environment.

How are we to assess these different re-interpretations of the importance of mothering? Is Chodorow voluntaristic and Rustin realistic? Or is Chodorow taking a historian's position and Rustin a biologistic stance? It is a merit of both that they discuss the psychoanalytic arguments in the context of social, cultural and ideological considerations but we would argue that, ultimately, neither goes far enough in this direction. Indeed, perhaps the major difficulty with psychoanalytic approaches in general is that they do not provide a sufficiently *social* contextualization of the familial processes they deal with.

We can examine this further by returning to the question of whether psychoanalysis does give an accurate description of

[84] 'A Socialist Reconsideration of Kleinian Psychoanalysis', *New Left Review*, 131 (January–February 1982), p. 87.

contemporary subjective reality. There is now a certain amount of consensus on the proposition that socialization based on paternal authority within the family has weakened. The law of the father is increasingly flouted. Recognition of this historical change has come from a variety of different political positions, and the debate over its consequences has tended to centre on moral evaluations of this 'collapse' of patriarchal authority. What must be emphasized, however, is that we cannot focus exclusively on processes internal to the family, as this will entirely mislead us into the blind alley of believing that 'the family' is in decline. As we have argued, dominant themes of familialism – including the authority relations identified by psychoanalysis – are absolutely pervasive in ideology generally. One way of putting this is to say, as Benjamin does, that patriarchal authority is now 'generalized' rather than 'personal' – the spirit of the culture.[85] It is irrelevant to mourn the death of the family when our society is more profoundly 'familialized' than ever before.

We do not see the familialization of society as taking a precisely patriarchal form. The ideology of familialism rests to some extent, certainly, on the social power of fatherhood, but it also encodes themes not precisely identified by the term 'patriarchy'. Women's dependence, generalized male power, normative endorsements of a broader sexual division of labour and so on play a part in an ideology of familialism that cannot be restricted to a specific concern with the father. In this sense, although we recognise the patriarchal dimensions of familial ideology, we do not see it as a phenomenon that the concept of patriarchy – with its specific emphasis on the father – can adequately summarize.

Psychoanalysis has proved extremely controversial for feminism, partly as a result of the debate over its political implications. We believe that this has led to an underemphasis on the extent of the cultural hegemony of familial ideology. Although it is important to look at the construction of gendered subjectivity within families and through child-rearing

[85] 'Authority', p. 56.

practices, it is crucial to recognize the broader ideological and cultural construction of gendered subjectivity. 'The family', as we have argued earlier, is not merely an economic unit, nor merely a kinship structure; it is also an ideological configuration with resonance far beyond these narrow definitions. For this reason, the increased interest in analysing the cultural representation of familialism is an extremely important development. Sociological approaches to 'the family' as a unit counterposed to 'society' tend to miss the crucial dimension of the ideological structuring of familialism. Film and media studies, in the past rather isolated from sociology of the family, have a considerable amount to contribute here. To illustrate this, we may cite a point made by Charlotte Brunsden in her analysis of the British television serial *Crossroads*: 'the action of the soap-opera is not restricted to familial or quasi-familial institutions but, as it were, *colonizes* the public masculine sphere, representing it from the point of view of the personal.'[86] This remark is incisively accurate. We have to engage with the ways in which the supposedly private sphere of the family is in fact better analysed as anything but private. Familialism pervades not merely 'women's' soap-opera but virtually every cultural genre. The television news could easily be subjected to an analysis in these terms, as could any public discourse. We need not merely an analysis of family-as-institution or family-as-socialization, we need an analysis of the utterly hegemonic status of the familial perspective and familial ideology. We dissent most strongly, therefore, from those who argue that 'the family' is in decline. We have stressed the anti-social character of the present form of the family but also the social privilege that makes it such a powerful entity. It is on the basis of our assessment of the strength, rather than the weakness, of familialism that we now turn to the question of strategies for change.

---

[86] '"Crossroads" - Notes on Soap Opera', *Screen*, vol. 22, no. 4, 1981.

IV
Strategies for Change

Abolition of the family! Even the most
radical flare up at this infamous
proposal of the communists.
COMMUNIST MANIFESTO

We have repeatedly stressed that the family presents certain advantages *within the context* of a particular society. In effect, we have tried simply to advance an explanation as to why the family is as popular as it is without really questioning how the family came to take this form, or why. The exercise is a salutary one, for often we fail to distinguish, in thinking about the family, between investment in an existing situation and an analytic knowledge that the situation itself could be different. We have, here, left in suspension the evolution and functions of the family as they are normally analysed, since we regard these as issues that often blind us to the very real needs met by it in its present form. Furthermore, answers to the question as to what people gain from the family now may shed new light on the question of how this family form has emerged as so dominant.

The conflation of these two aspects of analysing the family is a common problem, one that could be labelled 'functionalism'. In this context the danger of functionalism is that the style of analysis tends to ignore, as does conspiracy theory, dimensions of the family not immediately explicable as serving the interest of a particular ruling class or sex. Both Marxist and feminist accounts of the family can be charged, all too often, with this weakness – which is not merely an academic error or a sign of intellectual coarseness, but has serious political consequences.

The Marxist tradition has provided us with a trenchant critique of the family under capitalism. It is an agency of socialization, a key institution for the reproduction of capitalist ideology and capitalist social relations. It is a vehicle for the inheritance of private property and a mechanism for class placement. The present form of family is a distinctive variant developed by the emergent bourgeoisie and imposed upon a proletariat that did not independently develop the values of domesticity and dependence enshrined within it. Many of these arguments, much of this critique, we would endorse. Yet socialists putting forward the 'radical critique of the family' have found themselves increasingly isolated. The working class in its organized form has expressed considerable support for the family, has fought to protect it and improve its standard of living. It has not spoken out with a united voice against the inheritance by the son of the father's craft apprenticeship, nor has it expressed indignation at the double standard of sexual morality. Socialists who argued against these things were forced into considering the working class as suffering from 'false consciousness' in a mass, which is thought to be a patronizing stance. So it is small wonder that socialists have long back-pedalled on the critique of the family in the face of these accusations.

Feminism can be said to have suffered a similar fate. In seeing the family as the site of male attempts to control and exploit women, in arguing that heterosexuality and marriage are instruments of male power, feminists have encountered considerable hostility and resistance from women in general. Many women today will support general demands for rights and independence, but they simultaneously distance themselves from the 'anti-family, anti-men' extremism they see as characteristic of women's liberation as a political movement.

As Marxists and as feminists we are then faced with a difficult choice. Do we retain the integrity of our critique, or compromise in favour of more popular appeal and hope to reach a point when the critique will slowly take on more plausibility? It may be helpful to try and break down the barriers that have emerged between popular support for family life and a radical, intellectual critique of it as an oppressive ideology. To do so we would need to recognize that the iniquities of the family and its appeal are closely related – they are two sides of the same coin. The benefits of family life depend upon the suffering of those who are excluded. The *ideal* of the family life brings in its train many a bitter marriage and disappointed parents. If the family were not the only source of a range of satisfactions, were it not so massively privileged, it would not be so attractive.

The needs and satisfactions to which we refer – affection, security, intimacy, sexual love, parenthood and so on – are not artificial. We see these as human needs, not pathological constructs. The form in which they are currently met, however, we regard as both unsatisfying and anti-social. The purpose of our critique of this 'anti-social family' is not to demonstrate the imbecility of ideologically impregnated individuals, as Donzelot might fear. Nor is it to remove warmth and emotional fulfilment from the lives of the politically correct. Its purpose is to demonstrate the need for social and political change so that such needs and desires can be met in a more genuinely social context.

Changes of this sort cannot be wrought overnight. In the long term we are pursuing a major social transformation that will displace the family as the sole and privileged provider of moral and material support and spread these good things more widely through the community. In the short term, though, we cannot demand the immediate abolition of an institution that does meet real needs as well as being ultimately anti-social. A good example of this contradiction is the problem of ending the dependence of women on their husbands. Should we argue that men should no longer support their wives, that pension schemes should not provide for widows, that divorced women have no right to support from their ex-husbands? In the long term undoubtedly we should. But in the present situation, if women cannot escape the responsibility for housekeeping and caring for children and, even if they do work outside the home, can seldom earn as much as men, then any proposals we make must not be ones that would leave such women without the little shred of compensation that they now have. Nevertheless, we must work towards ending women's dependence: personal dependence is only a partial compensation, an unsatisfactory one, and one not available to all.

A similar contradiction can be seen in the problem of achieving full social responsibility for children. At the moment, since parents bear most of the work and costs of bringing up children, they expect to have the right to decide how they shall be brought up, and many see this as a natural feature of parenthood. Increases in social control are seen as interventions into private life and indeed this is the form they currently take. The social services departments of local authorities, the health visitors, the school welfare officers, are scarcely the agencies that socialists have in mind when we call for greater social responsibility for children. Nevertheless, we must refuse to accept the easy logic of parents' rights and must work towards greater social care and support of children, and greater social, rather than individual, control.

Two General Aims
In our view there are two general aims for political strategy on the family: (1) we should work for immediate changes that will increase the possibilities of *choice* so that alternatives to the existing favoured patterns of family life become realistically available and desirable; (2) we should work towards collectivism and away from individualism in the areas at present allocated to the sphere of private family life, especially income maintenance, the work of making meals, cleaning and housekeeping, and the work of caring for people such as children, the old and the sick or disabled.

Before we can discuss what these principles mean in practice for the various aspects of the politics of the family, it is necessary to say a little about the philosophical problems involved in concepts of 'collectivism' and 'choice'. A good way into this is to look at feminist and socialist debates about abortion rights.

To speak of extending people's right to choose smacks of the bourgeois individualism for which feminism has often been derided. It is said that to demand the right to choose between pursuing a profession and staying at home to care for children is all very well for the bourgeois woman, but meaningless for the working-class woman who must in any case work herself to exhaustion, both inside and outside the home and for whom employment is a necessary evil rather than personal fulfilment. Or it is said that the demand for 'a woman's right to choose' to have an abortion or not is fine for the bourgeois woman who can afford to have either the abortion or the baby as she chooses, but is inadequate for the poorer woman who needs access to free abortion, not merely the legal right to choose, and who needs time, money, help and house-room if the choice to have a baby is to be a real one. As Denise Riley has put it: ' "The right to choose" must imply the right to choose to have (not merely *not* to have) children, and this right is a very metaphysical assertion in a situation where provisions for the myriad needs for bringing up those children in a humane way are thin on the ground. And, of course, conspicuously thinner for some than for others. To follow through the "positive" aspect of the right to choose would entail a many-faceted campaign, a generalizing of the issue which linked it to a wider context of agitation for the reforms necessary to give more plausibility to the notion of choice.' But she continues: 'Nevertheless, it seems to me to be wrong to criticize an essentially defensive slogan, so heavily marked by its necessary strategic location, on the grounds of its incompleteness.'[1] Clearly, when we talk of choice, we must mean something more than purely formal legal freedom; we mean viable possibilities as well.

But there is a more fundamental risk of bourgeois individualism in the simple demand for the 'right to choose' in private life: that is, acceptance of the bourgeois distinction between public and private, between production and reproduction. Writing again of the campaign to retain abortion rights, Sue Himmelweit asked: 'Are we accepting that under socialism, or whatever name we give the society we are working for, production will be planned, ever so democratically, but

---

[1] Denise Riley, 'Feminist Thought and Reproductive Control: the State and the "Right to Choose" ', in Cambridge Women's Studies Group, eds., *Women in Society: Interdisciplinary Essays*, London 1981, p. 191.

planned for the benefit of all, but reproduction will remain a private, individual decision and right?' She, like Denise Riley, goes on to say, 'I raise these questions not because I believe that under the present climate and the present threats we have any choice but to wage a defensive struggle to claim the little areas of freedom that the present system has partially granted us and now threatens to take away.'[2] Even if we accept Marx's critique of Malthusian population theories, we must believe that a socialist society might wish to control its population growth or size. At its best this could involve collective decision-making by local groups of women as has been claimed for the anti-natalist policies of Maoist China. At its worst it could involve the peremptory removal of access to abortion, as in the pro-natalist Romanian policy of 1966. In between, it can involve structuring economic incentives, welfare and nursery provision or whatever in such a way as to attempt to influence what women choose. But in one way or another, socialism is bound to give a positive value to collective rather than individual concerns in questions of reproduction. What socialists must do is not *deny the existence* of individual rights, for these will surely exist and even flourish in socialist society, but *challenge the private content* attributed to such rights in bourgeois thought.

So political philosophy alerts us to the limited nature of demands for freedom of choice and the dangers of resting our analysis on a pure liberal individualism.[3] And the philosophy of mind may alert us to deeper problems in any ultimate conceptualization of what a pure choice could be or what the implications of positing a freely choosing subject might be. Yet again, as Denise Riley has written, 'it is nevertheless the case that the uncertain speech of the philosophy of "rights" is the chief inherited discourse – whatever its deficiencies – for the

---

[2] Sue Himmelweit, 'Abortion: Individual and Social Control', *Feminist Review*, no. 5, 1980, p. 66.

[3] The most advanced liberals are well aware of these problems too. For instance, T.H. Marshall recognized that equal formal citizenship gave full rein to substantive inequalities. *Citizenship and Social Class*, Cambridge 1950; see also Juliet Mitchell, 'Women and Equality', Mitchell and Oakley, eds., *The Rights and Wrongs of Women*, pp. 379–99.

framing of *any* demands for social reform or revolution. And demands for rights and choices are the expression of a critical refusal to leave the powers of decision to external authorities, be they doctors or government. The political significance of this refusal must override objections to "the right to choose" which are based only on the slogan's apparent implications of a free individual operating on an uncircumscribed terrain, in an idealism of isolated "choice". For while "choice" is obviously a complex concept, and while the right in law and in social policy to "make a choice" is by no means the whole story, nonetheless that right, minimal enough, is of a critical importance.'[4]

The theories of Michel Foucault have been used to deflate simplistic views of sexual liberation which depend upon a notion of a sexual being subjected to external repression. As Athar Hussain puts it: 'The lofty and noble projects of linking sexual liberation with political revolution – a not uncommon theme in left writings on sexuality – come in for withering mockery. Sexual liberation, Foucault claims, is an illusory horizon created by a mistaken view of power which comes to bear on sexuality.'[5] The workings of power are more complex than this; they cannot be understood as repression versus freedom or repression versus some rebellious, polyvalent sexual instinct. Nevertheless, the notion of liberation needs to be defended. The idea of repression may indeed be merely a way of talking of sexuality that has developed in the last two centuries, but some situations are more repressive and others more free. The attribution of, say, homosexuality as a personal identity may well be a phenomenon of those cultures often called 'anti-homosexual', but homosexual liberation, the right to claim that identity and engage in those activities, is still an important freedom to be won.

Personal Politics – Making Choices

There are many changes in law and institutions that we should

[4] Ibid., pp. 191–2.
[5] Athar Hussain, 'Foucault's *History of Sexuality*', *m/f*, nos. 5 & 6, p. 169.

fight for to give us a context of greater choice. But first we need to examine what we should do within the choices available to us now. For 'life-style politics' and the struggle to develop prefigurative forms of cooperative activity in the bosom of an often hostile society have long been an important strand of our political tradition, and rightly so. Time and again, feminist thought has rejected life-long monogamy, especially as imposed by marriage laws. Drawing on ideas that go back at least as far as the bohemians of the 1920s but came most immediately through the hippies of the 1960s, early women's liberationists set up households that rejected the conventions of bourgeois morality and sought to revalorize personal life by breaking down the boundaries of public and private. In the early 1970s there were feminist households where all doors had been removed, where people slept in whichever room had spare bed-space, and wore whichever clothes were to hand. More recently some feminists, despairing of transforming their relations with men, have turned to separatism, living as far as possible without the help or company of men. Most of us would not want to live in this way and do not accept the arguments in its favour. But we should defend the right of these women to do so.

Unfortunately, also, such projects have often been sustained by a moral righteousness that makes them distasteful to others. Separatists accuse women who live with men of 'loving their enemy'. People who believe in multiple relationships deride as politically backward those who feel the need of a primary partner. Life-style politics has fallen into disrepute partly because it so often claims to be *the* way: it claims that everyone should adopt the new way of life to bring about the revolution and it claims that this change in everyone's practice is all that is required. The Red Collective in London was one of the few groups to reject both these claims quite explicitly. A group of five women and men who each had some sexual relationships within the group, they sought to change the form of their relationships and to break down their one-to-one character. But they did not expect to inaugurate a new way of living just by an act of will. 'The particular structures of relationships that we have in the group are. . . not seen as an end which we have been trying to achieve as such, but as a context in which we have been trying to carry out changes in the way we relate.'[6] They recognized that the patterns of intimate relations are deep within us, that they are not just a habit of conformity to an alien bourgeois morality but involve needs and defences that are set up in childhood. At the same time they recognized that the isolation of families and the form of the couple relationship are structured by their place in a wider society. They expressed this in general terms by saying: 'Because capitalism imposes a separation between the sphere of commodity production and the sphere of consumption and the domestic economy, economic relations coincide with emotional ones in a very particular way within the family.'[7] But they also saw that changes in such things as housing provision, abortion law, child-care arrangements, and women's chances to earn good wages would open up more possibilities for changing the domestic economy and sexual relations. Even the existing social institutions do not determine unalterable family forms. The nuclear family, they argue, is an untheorized practice which emerged in the context of capitalist development. A conscious, theorized practice that would challenge the personal and the social relations of capitalism is a possible and necessary part of broader mass struggles.

If we must avoid the counterproductive stance of self-righteous moralizing, we must also avoid the defeatist stance of colluding with existing family morality on the grounds that it is too hard to change or cannot be changed on its own. It is important to work at the development of shared ideas towards a better way of living together. Perhaps one of the best of the varied meanings of the slogan 'the personal is political' is the idea of public discussion about personal life. This does not mean that our intimate relationships must be enacted on a public stage, but that the principles on which they are

---

[6] Red Collective, *The Politics of Sexuality in Capitalism*, London 1978, p. 41 (originally published as a pamphlet in 1973).
[7] Ibid., p. 61.

conducted and the conditions surrounding them should be a regular part of general political discussion.[8] It is in this spirit that we propose some basic principles of daily political struggle in personal life.

1. *Encourage variety.* Shulamith Firestone, who saw the oppression of women as rooted in the 'tyranny of reproductive biology' and fed by the economic dependence of women and children on a man and their isolation from the wider society, argued for flexibility in life-styles, for a programme of multiple options existing simultaneously, so that people could choose what suited them at different periods of their lives.[9] She thought there should be more possibilities for being single, which she rather quaintly associated with 'single professions', more ways of 'living together' without marriage, whether in sexual or non-sexual arrangements, and a developed system of larger 'households' where children could grow up. Her blueprint for these households involves shared child-care, shared chores, full membership rights for children, no ownership of children, a limited contract with the possibility of transfer to another household. Such households would exist alongside the single and group non-reproductive life styles giving a range of choice. Though her households are very similar to what are usually known as 'communes', she would clearly not accept the goal of many involved in British communes of transforming the whole of society into a federation of communes.

It is easy, perhaps, to dream up a variety of alternatives to the family or ways of eliminating the oppressive aspects of family life, such as the 'open marriage',[10] or the 'open family'.[11] It is even easier to ridicule other people's dreams.

---

[8] This we assume is the impulse behind the pamphlets recently written by two left-wing Labour activists: Chris Knight, *My Sex Life*, and Ann Bliss, *Our Sex Lives – Our Strength*, London Labour Briefing, 1980.

[9] *The Dialectic of Sex*, London 1979, pp. 212–21.

[10] Nena O'Neill and George O'Neill, *Open Marriage: New Life-styles for Couples*, New York 1972.

[11] L.L. Constantine, 'Open Family: A Life-style for Kids and Other People', *The Family Co-ordinator*, April 1977, pp. 113–21; reprinted in Michael Anderson, ed., *Sociology of the Family*, second edn. Harmondsworth 1980.

Women separatists cannot cope with men and are living in a cosy regressive nursery. Communes have done little to transform gender relations and nothing to break down the mother-child bond.[12] The open family boasts of children's rights, but at the whim of the parents.[13] Homosexual couples either become purely domestic, seeking sex outside, or else ape marriage (or sometimes both). Experimentation with new ways of living is a form of petty-bourgeois protest against alienating occupations and the suburban nuclear family.[14] But sneering at what others are trying to do is too easy. They are bound to be idealistic, infantile, crypto-reactionary or insufficiently radical. What purpose does such criticism serve? It can be constructive and a valuable part of a political commitment to change. Or it can be a justification for settling down, after some youthful experimentation, into a conventional family mode. The thoughtful article that Philip Abrams and Andrew McCulloch wrote about 'Women, Men and Communes'[15] is often invoked to dismiss all attempts to transcend the family. Yet if the commune movement is a form of petty-bourgeois protest, then socialists should be glad their protest has taken this progressive direction. We should welcome it, engage with it, try to understand its class nature, but also help it to develop beyond that.

Many of us in and around the women's liberation movement choose to live alone or else in households that are not formed on the family model. There is by now a wealth of experience of the many problems involved. Sharing housework, cooking or

[12] Philip Abrams and Andrew McCulloch, 'Men, Women and Communes', in Diana Barker and Sheila Allen, eds., *Sexual Divisions and Society*, London 1976.
[13] Constantine (ibid.) describes the effect on him of reading R. Farson, *Birthrights: A Bill of Rights for Children*, New York 1974: 'The book really raised my consciousness and I proposed to Joan that we were usurping some of the kids' rights and making excess work for ourselves. It seem a bit silly now, but Joan and I discussed it for months before cautiously proposing to the kids a new *modus operandi* at bedtime.' He still refers to them as 'my own kids'.
[14] Abrams and McCulloch; Constantine refers to T. Gordon's *Parent Effectiveness Training*, New York 1970, as a 'no-lose model of parent-child relationships', which suggests that 'open families' may be a fantasy solution to authority problems typical of petty-bourgeois households.
[15] Abrams and McCulloch.

child-care is not easy, especially for people brought up in families where all this was controlled by one woman. The loss of control and absence of established norms and patterns of trust can engender a sense of insecurity. The decision to have children may have to be made in the context of uncertainty about who will enjoy rights and who will shoulder responsibilities. Households can break up amidst resentment and recrimination. Yet living in these various ways that challenge the family is often rewarding and enjoyable. Children brought up more collectively are at least as sane and independent as their peers. Friendships and love relationships are less clearly demarcated and can be enduring and remarkably supportive. Heterosexual and homosexual ways of life merge and learn from one another. We may not ourselves wish or feel able to be radically innovative in our personal lives. But we should encourage variety by supporting others who do. If others work at communal living, shared child-care, shared housework, celibacy, non-parenthood (how strange we have nothing but clumsy words for it: childlessness?), homosexuality that does not mirror heterosexual patterns, the least we can do is support them. We should not undermine their efforts, but engage with them constructively.

2. *Avoid oppressive relationships.* The idea of love has a lot to answer for. In its name, people who are otherwise rational and socially perceptive walk as if spellbound into traps and prisons. How often has a male lecturer having a relationship with a student, or a doctor with a nurse, or a manager with a typist, been heard to say, 'our relationship is not like that; she is really a strong, mature person; we are breaking down status barriers; we are absolutely equal'? Of course. In love the partners are equal. But in every other aspect of their relationship – at parties, in discussions, in money, in arguments – they are inevitably unequal, gender being reinforced by hierarchy. How often have people succumbed to the argument, 'if you really loved me you wouldn't mind marrying me, despite your theoretical and principled objections to marriage; what harm can a bit of paper do to a relationship between people? It only

sets a seal on what we feel anyway'? Of course. But it also endows the relationship with respectability and social privilege and thereby devalues all other relationships. It is the end of the woman's economic independence as far as tax, social security and a pattern of welfare benefits are concerned. And when love is over, the shell of the relationship endures, and to break out of it a whole machinery of law must be invoked. How often have mothers (though seldom fathers) said, 'I am enjoying the new baby so much, I don't think I'll go back to work straight after my maternity leave'? Of course, caring for a baby can be a delight. But such women usually also take over the housework and cooking from that time on. And when they do look for a job again they can only find one that is less good than the one they left. How often have women said, 'my husband's career means he has to work long hours, so I have a part-time job and look after the house'; or, 'I gave up my job when his father had a stroke and came to live with us; that was twelve years ago'? Of course, loving care for a partner and his family are fine. But in its name women become trapped in the household and unable to support themselves. Sometimes there is no choice open to us, but too often we take the easy conforming path without considering where it leads.

As well as being clear-eyed about what we are doing and trying to rethink our own relationships and households, we should be aware of the social impact of what we do. Each woman who is coquettish with men and each mother who indulges her child with excessive attention and toys makes it harder for other women to resist the pressures from men and children. 'No man is an island', despite the cultural view that personal life is a purely private matter of consequence only to those involved.

Marriage is an oppressive institution for both the married and the unmarried, and provides the major legal support for the current family form. We believe that socialists and feminists should not get married themselves and should not attend or support the marriages of any who can be convinced of our critique of the family. 'Paper' marriages designed to get round immigration restrictions may perhaps be an exception.

But savings to be made on income tax or death duties are no excuse: that is a form of collusion, not of subversion. Distress to older relatives is scarcely ever an excuse: only twenty years ago such distress would have been acute in most sections of British society, yet many young people were courageous enough to follow their own beliefs and marriage is a weaker institution in consequence. There are very few cultures within British society where the young should not be beginning to take this stand. As Diana Leonard Barker put it: 'For a "companionate", sexually libertarian couple to undergo the [wedding] ceremony is, at the very least, a recognition of the continuing power of their parents, the community, the church and socially structured sex roles. . . . Our feminist ire should not be aroused by the apparent anachronism of the rituals but by what they confirm and tell us about the continuing characteristics of marriage as an institution.'[16] Of course, just resisting formal marriage itself does not guarantee that we escape from a marital type of relationship. In Sweden, for instance, cohabitation has become common among younger couples. Yet it is said that their relations often give them household presents when they set up home together, and they seem to have become assimilated to the old patterns. Similarly, even swapping roles between a man and a woman can produce a mirror-image couple that does more to confirm the recognized pattern than to challenge it.

Nobody should have a housewife. Nobody, man, child, invalid, or woman, needs a long-term 'housewife' or has the right to have one. Unpaid domestic service is in principle inferior to social provision. For those who can afford it, paying someone to clean the house or cook meals is preferable to making it the duty of one household member. Many socialists have qualms about this, without being very clear about why. What is wrong with it is not that someone else is doing your dirty work – after all, if you believe it should be socialized, you believe that it is not eternally *your* private responsibility. What is wrong is that someone, usually a woman, is being paid an

16 'A Proper Wedding', p. 77.

abysmally low wage and that the relation is one of mistress-and-servant. It should be more like engaging a plumber and less like having a skivvy. As long as we must all do our own housework on the same scale, women are essentially no more capable of housework than men. Men have deskilled themselves in order to get out of it and women have colluded in order to gain some pride in compensation for a disadvantaged situation. By the same token, women are no more innately gifted for intensive child-care than men. So child-care should be shared between men and women. And it should not be shared on the basis of contrasting styles: when men care for children they should do it in the warm, intimate way that only women usually have – allowing children to show their vulnerability, comforting and cuddling, rather than just romping and joking, as men have so often done. Women, too, should feel able to have fun with children, rather than only 'looking after' them. Men should also recognize that being involved with children means being responsible: you cannot make plans to go out without considering what will happen to them. Such responsibility need not be the burden it is for isolated little families at present. This is why feminists have long campaigned for more social forms of care. We cannot rely on redistributing existing tasks within existing households, important though this is; we must also try to socialize them and find alternative ways of carrying them out. The problem with this at present is that these alternatives are often not available or are unappealing or too expensive.

The women's movement has articulated the resentment underlying women's, often graceful, resignation to the role of housewife and mother; more and more women are aware of what a sacrifice it is. Men who have housewives have more energy to devote to their careers or to working odd hours or overtime. They get on well, but at the expense of others and women who have no houseperson.

These are not ideas that will make life miserable, but ideas for happier living. Though they are mainly aimed at undermining the guarantees of male privilege, they also pave the way for forming new kinds of household that are more rewarding for all involved.

3. *Beware of domesticity.* The Red Collective wrote of one unreconstructed relationship that it was 'a basis from which the man can act on the outside world but which absorbs the woman into the couple'.[17] A danger may be that in re-constructing our relationships, in devoting ourselves to the politics of the personal, we may all become absorbed into the couple or into the household. This is more likely to happen where a couple live together without other adults. One simple antidote is that each person should have their own space within the household – 'a room of one's own'. Cramped housing makes this impossible for most people. Yet many who have the space, and can afford to heat it, still seem to use it in such a way that they live in each other's pockets. The television that the children watch is in the only comfortable living room. The woman does her sewing at the dining-table, though there is a whole room upstairs designated as a 'spare bedroom'. The sharing of a marital bedroom is considered essential, despite snoring, sickness or insomnia. The open-plan living space enhances family 'togetherness' and demands a high level of involvement in family life. Anyone who has friends in must share them with the whole family.

We are not arguing against personal life, or against privacy, but for a better balance between private and public and a private life that is not so demanding and draining and not so all-important. For many people, work is so unrewarding that they centre their lives around the home. Decorating the home, furnishing it, equipping it with gadgetry become major act-ivities. Family leisure and a child-centred life-style become the sources of their deepest satisfaction. Public spaces become shopping precincts where people go only to stock up on the goodies they consume in private. As every socialist knows, it becomes almost impossible to attract a decent crowd to a public meeting.

[17] Red Collective, p. 41.

To some extent the solution must involve changing the nature of work, and 'revitalizing public life'.[18] As Alexandra Kollontai wrote, 'the stronger the collective, the more firmly established becomes the communist way of life. The closer the emotional ties between the members of the community, the less the need to seek refuge from loneliness in marriage.'[19] Nevertheless there is much that we can do in our own lives to resist pressures towards cosy domestic self-sufficiency and the privileging of home life. This is not without its problems, since the less conventional our household arrangements the more we become cut off from ordinary people and thrown back on each other. But we can at least beware of the Scylla of home improvements, domestic comforts and security without getting psychologically wrecked by the Charybdis of squalor, isolation and impersonality.

We have presented these three principles – encourage variety, avoid oppressive relationships, beware domesticity – in a spirit of opening up discussion. We have put forward our own views, but we do not intend to preach a rigid pattern of moral rectitude to everyone else. We do, however, believe that changes in our own lives are possible and that everyone should be working on the kinds of questions we have outlined.

Some Changes to Fight For

It is in the light of the two guiding aims of greater freedom of choice and the move towards collectivism that feminist and socialists should judge current proposals on social policy as they affect the family. At present all of us, and especially the poor, are constrained to forms of personal life that are

---

[18] The phrase is Marshall Colman's in *Continuous Excursions*, London 1982. He, however, sees it as an alternative to life-style politics, arguing that, 'Personal politics has become identified with a minority life-style, at times so bizarre that it has little hope of affecting ordinary people. Instead of concerning itself with the way that a *few* people live, it should concern itself with the way most people live, and should turn to the revitalization of public life.'

[19] Alix Holt, ed., *Alexandra Kollontai: Selected Writings*, London 1977, p. 231.

privatized in families. There are few available alternatives, and the alternatives that do exist are inferior and stigmatized. Those who have managed to choose and establish other ways of living have tended to be better off, or else willing to put up with considerable material privation. A key strategy, then, must be to change all the state policies that currently privilege 'the family' at the expense of other ways of living.

This does not mean attacking families or people who live in them. But it does mean cutting through the common political cant about the family as 'the basic unit of society' and the need to 'strengthen the stability and quality of family life'. In practice, those who most fervently preach the organic role of the family do least when in power to help family members.[20] For what they are defending is precisely a family that will look after itself, whose members will not turn elsewhere for care or support, self-sufficient, self-contained, selfish.

Here we can only set out what we see as the major changes we should be fighting for in the near future. Some of them are well established as feminist or socialist demands. On others there is less agreement and more need for debate. They revolve around weakening all the pressures that compel people to live or stay in nuclear family households, especially the pressures of financial need and of the need to be looked after, but also including moral and cultural pressures.

Wages. As long as we live in a system where the wage is the main way in which people's needs are met, wages should be large enough to support those who work for them. This means that women and young people should be able to earn a wage that does not assume they live as a dependant in someone else's household. For women, this means a great deal more than 'equal pay for equal work': it means some kind of positive action to change the whole way work is organized.[21] Women

---

[20] Jean Coussins and Anna Coote, *The Family in the Firing Line*, Poverty Pamphlet No. 51, London 1981.

[21] Angela Weir and Mary McIntosh, 'Towards a Wages Strategy for Women', *Feminist Review*, no. 10, 1982.

should not be confined to 'women's jobs', and women's jobs should not be defined as less skilled and demanding than men's. Women should have equal chances of training and promotion and equal chances of working overtime or obtaining other perks. Time off to care for children should not condemn anyone to the worst and least secure jobs. Maternity leave should be extended to cover anyone caring for small babies during the day. None of this can be done without changing men's situation. They will lose some privileges; they will also gain the opportunity to take a period off paid work for child-care, or to work shorter hours so that they can shop and cook, without spoiling their career. They will lose the right to assume they should earn a 'family wage' to support a wife and children; they will also gain freedom from the obligation to be a breadwinner.[22]

If young people or women can earn a living wage as individuals they are not bound to their parents or their husband by financial need. They are free to come and go and to form relationships that are not mercenary and in which they have more of a say. A man who is no longer the main breadwinner will begin to lose some of his power as father and husband.

Social Security. Not everyone can earn a wage; children cannot and, for the forseeable future, women will spend more time out of employment than men. They should not have to be dependent on their husbands. Social security provision should not be based on the assumption that family members will support each other. This leads to gross inequalities. Families with children are in general poorer than those without; so are families with only one person earning. Yet it is when children are young that their mothers find it hardest to work outside the home. Clearly an adequate child benefit is needed, at a level commensurate with what it costs to keep a child. In Britain a universal child benefit already exists in principle, but so far it

---

[22] Michèle Barrett and Mary McIntosh, 'The Family Wage: Some Problems for Socialists and Feminists'. *Capital and Class*, no. 11, 1980.

has not begun to match what children actually cost. Then we need an adequate income for women whether or not they are in employment and whether or not they are living with a man. In Britain at present women have similar National Insurance rights to men (though it will not be until 1984 that they will be able to claim benefits for their dependent children on the same basis as men). But as far as non-insured benefits are concerned (and once insured sickness or unemployed benefits have run out), married and cohabiting women are treated as their husband's dependant. They cannot have an invalidity pension unless they are incapable of housework as well as paid work; they cannot claim an allowance to stay at home and care for an invalid dependent relative; for means-tested benefits their resources and needs are 'aggregated' with those of their husband so that if he is earning they probably get no benefit. We need to move towards 'disaggregation'[23], so that married women have independent rights to social security on the same conditions as anyone else. The same principle should apply to income tax (and to capital transfer tax, where there should be no exemption for husbands and wives). The 'aggregation' of husband and wife in means-tested social security and in tax is the most important way that the state bolsters the marriage system; yet it does so quite often by putting married people at a disadvantage. Disaggregation would have immense effects on women's dependence. Many unemployed women become housewives, relying on their husbands for support. If they could claim a benefit in their own right, they would become unemployed people, seeking work and living on supplementary benefit meanwhile.

But means-tested benefits were originally intended as a residual safety-net; they are not appropriate for providing support for people whose earning capacity is cut by responsibility for caring for children or other dependants. Time out of

[23] Women's Liberation Campaign for Legal and Financial Independence and Rights of Women, 'Disaggregation Now! Another Battle for Women's Independence', *Feminist Review*, no. 2, 1979; Mary McIntosh, 'Feminism and Social Policy', *Critical Social Policy*, no. 1. 1981.

paid work for such care should be a risk covered by the ordinary National Insurance scheme. There has been dispute among feminists as to whether women should be paid an allowance for child-care. Some have even gone so far as to say all women should get 'wages for housework'. Others argue for a 'home responsibility payment' for anyone, man or woman, who stays at home to care for small children or for the old or disabled. The advantage here is that this is hard work that is seldom recognized as important and useful, and that, if it were paid for, many women would be released from economic dependence. The disadvantage is that they might become more firmly trapped, instead, in 'womanly' duties to home and family, as the proposal effectively privileges individual family child-care. If the allowance were really enough to live on, it would scarcely be worthwhile for such a woman to take a paid job, especially as she would then have to pay for some other form of child-care. One possibility that has been canvassed is that every pre-school child (or set of children) should have a child-care allowance which could be paid either to a parent staying at home or to a nursery or childminder. This would mean that nurseries and child-care would not, as the women's liberation movement has demanded, be provided free; yet everyone would be able to afford them. The payment would be a way of creating choice, and there is little doubt that we would find many more mothers opting for their children to be cared for in some collective way. The payment would also open up the possibility for all sorts of new nurseries and nursery schools, developing non-sexist and democratic styles.

A scheme like this might also be adapted to the care of the dependent disabled, with cash allowances covering either home or day-care centres or spells in residential care. In Britain, at least, the principle of a state 'attendance allowance' has been established; it needs to be extended.

Caring. Paying for the care of young children and the disabled drives a coach and horses through the old idea of the self-sufficient family. It recognizes caring as a collective responsibility and as a real social contribution, not just a natural expression of love and duty. But even more important is that such caring should become collectively organized and, as much as possible, take place in a lively and sociable setting, not shut away in isolated flats and houses. We need more and better nurseries and after-school play facilities, not only to help harassed mothers but also because they are more efficient and socially more stimulating and enriching. We need a better health service that can look after the chronically ill and the convalescent as well as acute hospital cases. We need day centres and residential care for everyone who cannot be left alone to look after themselves. The people who use these services should have a major say in deciding how they are run, so that they can really meet their needs.

But we also need collective provision to cover a lot of the everyday caring that women do within the family: housework, cooking, washing. Proper meals should be available at school and at work. There should be communal social centres where people can eat out and enjoy their leisure without spending a fortune. Pubs and restaurants should be more welcoming to people with children. There should be shared facilities for laundry and dry cleaning and shared machinery like industrial vacuums, sewing machines and lawn-mowers, making household work and gardening easier.

Housing. More modern housing can reduce the amount of drudgery and make housework easier. There is a danger that it can also raise standards and offer opportunities for even more elaborate arrangements for home-centred living.[24] But at least it can offer people greater choice about the way they live. At present too much of the good housing is geared to nuclear-family living. Housing managers tend to allocate the best council housing to 'good' families with a stable breadwinning father and relegate the single parents and other 'undesirables'

[24] Maxine Molyneux points out that it is often the poorest people, living in slums, hostels and shanties, who can do the least domestic labour and have to rely most on buying commercially the goods and services they need ('Beyond the Domestic Labour Debate', *New Left Review*, 116, 1979, pp. 10–11).

to poorer-quality dwellings.[25] Building societies are reluctant to give mortgages except to heads of families; they are not keen on households of unrelated adults, or even on dual-career couples. Housing cooperatives and associations, which in recent years have provided some accommodation for single people, are being squeezed financially, though the 'single homeless' are at last being recognized as a serious housing problem. The policy of increasing the amount of owner-occupation, at the expense of private and public rented accommodation, is specifically designed to bolster the family and the commitment to domestic life. In the present housing market, owning your own house is the best form of security; but it involves a great investment of money and time and ties you emotionally to the home. It gives residents greater control, but it tends to give that control to the man in the household, the one who can get a mortgage and afford to make the repayments. On divorce, for instance, the wife can now often claim the right to the home even if she did not pay for it, but she will often not be able to afford to go on living in it. In the private rented sector, socialists have long fought for security of tenure – yet it can be double-edged in a context of acute housing shortage, when you are secure only as long as you remain in the same family group. A woman who just chooses to leave her husband is not considered a priority for rehousing even if she has children; her husband, as the tenant, has security of tenure in their house or flat, so the council is reluctant to be responsible for housing both partners separately. Getting housed after separation or divorce has never been easy, but the new Housing Act may have made it even more difficult. So security of tenure must not be a socialist shibboleth; it must go alongside policies that make for greater freedom and flexibility in setting up and changing households.

Family Law. The increasing amount of divorce and single parenthood is making the whole field of family law a newly

---

[25] Most of the ideas in this section come from Helen Austerberry and Sophie Watson, 'A Woman's Place: A Feminist Approach to Housing in Britain', *Feminist Review*, no. 8, 1981.

154

problematic one. Some notable advances have been made in Britain in recent years. The Domestic Violence Act (1976) gives women much better protection against violent husbands; it has even – at last – been recommended that rape in marriage should be treated *as* rape and be punishable as a crime. Since 1969 divorce can be obtained by mutual consent, or after separation, without the idea of one party being innocent and the other guilty of a matrimonial offence of adultery, cruelty or desertion. This reform has thrown into question the obligation of one partner (almost always the husband) to maintain the other after a divorce or separation. There is a lobby on behalf of divorced men arguing that 'in these days of women's liberation' women should not expect marriage to be a 'bread ticket for life'. On the other hand, some feminists argue that since the husband has used his wife for unpaid labour during the marriage and she is disadvantaged in the labour market, he should pay her maintenance after divorce. Official opinion is very divided and the Law Commission recently produced a report[26] in which the pros and cons of seven different possible models for financial settlement on divorce were aired; one thing they seem fairly clear about is that a man ought to support his ex-wife if she would otherwise have to turn to the state for support. The problems are far from simple and are, of course, further complicated where there are young children.

Discussions in this area are too often couched in terms of abstract moral principles and do not take account of the realities of post-marital life. For instance the Supplementary Benefits Commission did a study which found that many women were claiming benefit because the maintenance order granted by the Court was below the state benefit level, and furthermore that 'payment of 40% of the maintenance orders fell into the category of less than 10% degree of regularity.'[27] It is no good ordaining that maintenance shall be paid if husbands cannot or will not pay and women have to turn to the state for support anyway. There is no way that justice can be

[26] *The Financial Consequences of Divorce: A Discussion Paper*, London 1980.
[27] *Report of the Committee on One-parent Families* (Finer Report), London 1974, vol. 1, pp. 99–100.

achieved between people who are so often fundamentally unequal. Nevertheless, our view is that the law should not simply assume married women's dependence – to do so would be to reinforce it – but should do everything to ease divorce and the formation of new households. So we favour the 'clean break' model of divorce where any property is divided as soon as possible and there is no continuing obligation to provide maintenance, except for children until they start work. However, this would need to be tempered by a recognition that women often are unable to support themselves, especially after a long period of marriage when they have kept house and worked outside only intermittently or part-time. The courts should be given guidelines on making protective settlements in such cases. Also, disposal of the marital home presents rather different problems from maintenance, though at present the two tend to be considered together. But in general principle we do not think that the inequality between men and women – differential wages and job opportunities – can be corrected by individual divorce settlements. Settlements in favour of individual women, such as the 'chivalrous' ones for which Lord Denning was famous, are not necessarily in the interests of women as a whole. As *The Cohabitation Handbook* puts it: 'Desirable as it is to improve matters, this is not the way to do it.'[28]

The same sort of thinking must guide us in disputes about the custody of children. But here the balance seems to us to fall the other way at present. Ultimately we are aiming to create a society in which men and women are equally involved in child-care, which will be in any case much less centred on parents. So a father, or indeed anyone else, who has really been equally involved in caring for a child has as much right to custody as a mother has. Nevertheless, we think that the usual current practice of the courts of awarding custody to the mother is the right one, simply because women nearly always have been the main parents and because the ideology of motherhood is so

---

[28] Anne Bottomley, Katherine Gieve, Gay Moon and Angela Weir, *The Cohabitation Handbook: A Woman's Guide to the Law*, London 1981, p. 117.

strong that they feel far more bereft, feel a greater sense of failure, if they are parted from their children. We do not accept the usual considerations that judges are guided by: that young children are naturally better off with their mother, that if the father has a new wife or lives with his mother his claim is stronger because he can offer a substitute mother, that a woman who is a lesbian has a weaker claim because she cannot provide a 'normal' environment.[29] But we do not think we have yet reached the stage where it would be helpful to ignore the sex of the parent and take only 'sex-blind' considerations into account. So, for the immediate future at least, each father must justify his claim to custody against a strong presumption of the mother's right. Anyone, whether a blood relative or not, should be able to claim custody on the basis that they have actually done the work of caring for the child.

Parents' Rights. We have already discussed some of the problems in the politics of abortion and contraception and argued that, at present, it is very important to defend parents' (and particularly mothers') right to choose whether or not to have children. For at present it really is parents who 'have' them and who must take on most of their support, care, rearing, training, as a private responsibility and more or less on their own. The time to start questioning whether bringing children into the world should be a purely individual decision will be when child-rearing is a much more collective enterprise.

To some extent, the same argument can be applied to parental rights over children. In principle, children are not the private property of their parents, so we should favour social rather than individual prerogatives over their lives. But this does not mean that the existing local authority children's departments should have the right to whisk children off into care whenever they disapprove of the way a mother runs her home, or that the existing schools should have the right to make children abandon the clothing of their ethnic minority or

---

[29] Julia Brophy and Carol Smart, 'From Disregard to Disrepute: the Position of Women in Family Law', *Feminist Review*, no. 9, 1981, p. 13.

submit to corporal punishment. The political problem at present is that these debates are, always couched in terms of parental rights versus state rights. In reality, the idea of parents' rights has grown up alongside the idea of parental responsibility for rearing the children the state needs. So parents are held responsible for preparing infants to start school, for ensuring the attendance and motivation of school children, for preventing delinquency and drug taking and generally for turning out hard-working and law-abiding citizens. Miriam David has argued that state policy relies upon a 'family-education couple' to reproduce the social and sexual division of labour.[30] In this context we should be striving to shift the parameters of the debate away from rights and towards responsibilities, away from *whose* responsibilities and towards responsibilities *to do what*.

Take for instance the right-wing argument for the 'right to choose' in education, which means that parents should be able to choose what sort of state school system there is and whether to send their children to private school. Firstly, it is worth pointing out that this 'right to choose' is often presented as opposition to outside interference: in fact it means parental control over children instead of social control. Then, the debate should properly not be about parental rights versus state rights but about whether it is better for the children of rich and ambitious parents to be sent to the 'best' schools while the children of the poor go to the nearest, or for the local education department to plan things so that each school has a mixture of background and ability and offers everyone the best possible opportunities.

Similarly, the debate about corporal punishment should not be over whether the school has the right to cane *my* child but over whether the use of the cane is a good thing, in school or out. Teachers should feel that they are responsible, not to parents, but to the community as a whole, for the way they treat the children. The recent ruling in the European Court, that a parent can insist on their child not being punished

[30] *The State, the Family and Education*, London 1980.

physically, will have the effect of abolishing corporal punishment in British schools. Although we agree with the end result, it would have been more progressive for this to have been achieved as a social decision rather than through the individualist rhetoric of parents' rights over the bodies of their children.

The issue of child-neglect and the role of the social worker raises perhaps more thorny questions. Even when it is suspected that young children are being battered by their parents, local authority social services departments are reluctant to remove the child from the home. The logic of our collectivist position might seem to be that the child may not be best off staying with its parents and that children should more often be taken into the care of the local authority. Yet social work also represents an intrusion into people's lives – and especially working-class lives. Through social workers and other professionals the state regulates family life, and the threat of the compulsory care order is only one instrument of control. Here again, then, we meet the problem of the rebarbative character of the existing class forms of collectivity. Yet here again we would argue that we must not retreat into the individualism of 'the family', but must fight for better kinds of collectivism. So we should recognize that at present we would often want to defend a parent's right to keep her child. But at the same time we should be working to improve the quality of children's homes, to open them up so that teenagers unhappy at home might actually *choose* to go to them or parents choose to send their younger children to them for a while without fear or stigma.

What Would You Put in Its Place?

Any critique of the family is usually greeted with, 'but what would you put in its place?' We hope that by now it will be clear that we would put nothing in the place of the family. Anything *in its place*, with the world around it unchanged, could probably be little different from the household patterns and ideology that we know as 'the family' at present. A society that offers few other sources of psychic security and little other means of material support is likely to throw people together into little defensive groups and to leave those who do not form such groups isolated and deprived. A male-dominated society is likely to produce a form of private life in which men are privileged and powerful. What is needed is not to build up an alternative to the family – new forms of household that would fulfil all the needs that families are supposed to fulfil today – but to make the family less necessary, by building up all sorts of other ways of meeting people's needs, ways less volatile and inadequate than those based on the assumption that 'blood is thicker than water'.

It is the belief that kinship, love and having nice things to eat are naturally and inevitably bound up together that makes it hard to imagine a world in which 'family' plays little part. This mythologized unity must be picked apart, strand by strand, so that we can understand its power and meet the needs of each of its separate elements more fully. In part, this can be done by analysis and discussion, as we have tried to do here. But it must also be done by experiments in new ways of living and by political campaigns to transform not the family – but the society that needs it.

Postscript
to Second Edition

The Anti-social Family was written ten years ago: the decade that has passed has made its general arguments more pertinent than ever. In the conclusion of the book we put forward a politics of *choice* and a call for a tolerant and pluralistic approach to personal life. Re-reading that chapter now, the tone and style seem strikingly didactic compared with what we are used to today. But it is worth emphasizing that the moralism involved was not the promulgation of some simple socialist or feminist orthodoxy. We were preaching a much more liberal creed: that individuals have some power to encourage diversity and to challenge oppressive institutions; and hence that we all have a duty not to collude in existing moralities and the imposition of rigid normative codes. We are now seeing signs in Britain of a more pragmatic and less doctrinaire approach to the politics of the family, and these changes serve to demonstrate just how coercive the years of high Thatcherism were.

Underlying the book's appeal for diversity and choice was a central argument against the individualism and privatism associated with an 'anti-social' family; in favour of encouraging collective and social means of satisfying personal needs. The transformation of Eastern Europe has called that vocabulary into question. In the Soviet bloc words like 'collectivism' and 'solidarity' are discredited by their association with the old authoritarian regime. For some in the West, the idea of socialism itself has been thrown into doubt by its failure in the East. Yet, paradoxically, at the same moment, the rise of green politics and environmentalism in the West has breathed new life into some of these old ideas. The market is quite obviously incapable of solving London's traffic problems, let alone global warming. In this context, collectivism and a sense of social responsibility have come to be seen as the only alternative to capitulation to the destructive logic of capitalism's drive towards local profit, whatever the longer-term global price.

Families and Social Inequality

The main substantive theses of *The Anti-social Family* are outlined in the second chapter. The onus on families to be providers of welfare for adults and children is a major way in which social inequalities are reproduced. This remains true, and we could take two instances where changes over the past decade have exacerbated the situation.

Increased 'parental choice' in education, and the devolution of responsibilities from local education authorities to individual schools, mean that parents have to search around for the best schools for their children: the affluent and mobile frequently move house to secure a better option and property values increasingly take this into account. Parents who cannot afford to play the schools market in this way, or who do not have the information on which to make such judgements, are likely to pass on the educational disadvantages they themselves suffered. But this time around it is 'their fault' that their children end up in poor schools where they do badly. The schools themselves, particularly in the hard-pressed inner cities, are under increasing pressure of resources and one response has been to involve parents further in their children's schoolwork, as well as in school finances and fund-raising. Otherwise progressive schemes, such as parents helping with motivation by regularly listening to children reading at home and liaising with the teacher about it, have clear class consequences. This can be fine for English-speaking educated parents with only one or two children and time to spend with them; for others it may be difficult to manage, a source of strain and guilt, or else completely alienating. So policies designed to help the overstretched teacher with too large a class have thrown the stress over onto families and, at the level of society as a whole, further reproduce inequalities in the next generation.

A second example would be the extension of home ownership. Two-thirds of British households are now owner-occupiers. Ostensibly, this is a progressive move that will favour the redistribution of wealth and support families by enabling people to live securely in their homes and build up an asset to leave to their children. But these benefits are dramatically affected by regional factors, by the timing of purchase in relation to housing values and borrowing costs, and by the variable loss of equity caused by parents having to finance their retirement and old age from the property. Furthermore, what of the one-third of households where children have no chance of inheriting? There is one group which is unlikely ever to inherit, and that is the children of today's tenants.[1] The question of inheritance tax rates and thresholds, which once related only to the rich, will become a substantial political issue as more first-generation homeowners die. It is an issue where ideas about family and class, about the perpetuation of privilege and the privileging of the private, will be very much in play.

The Anti-social Family also argues that the way in which family life is privileged makes it harder for people to live outside families. This is, if anything, more pertinent than it was a decade ago. There has been a significant increase in homelessness among single people in Britain. People of all ages sleep out in the centres of our large cities. The young who leave their parents' homes, the mentally ill whose hospitals are closed to make way for 'care in the community', people who become unemployed or whose marriages break down, are all casualties of a system that stresses self-reliance – meaning reliance on your family. Homelessness is but the starkest

[1] Chris Hamnet *et al.*, *Safe as Houses: Housing Inheritance in Britain*, London 1990.

of many images of life for those who find themselves outside
the family. Old people who have no kin to help them find
that the local home help services are inadequate and overstretched; migrant workers who have left their families behind
to work in British hotels and hospitals are subject to the most
appalling exploitation, as well as being victims of racist immigration laws; single mothers who have to try to extract maintenance for their children from their ex-husband or the
children's father, and so it goes on. But those who choose
voluntarily to live alternative lifestyles, or who are seeking
to challenge the hegemonic power of familialism, have also
been increasingly beleaguered in a climate of market individualism allied to moral conservatism.

Feminism, Racism and the Politics of the Family

Feminist politics have changed considerably since *The Anti-
social Family* was written. It is no longer possible to write
as if the category 'women' was an undifferentiated or unitary
one and as if 'women's interests' in a general sense could
readily be identified. In part, this is because of developments
in theory, which have recognized gender as a social and historical process and sought to deconstruct the categories of
'women' and 'men': undermining the apparently natural basis
of sisterhood between women. In part, it has been because
of developments in political practice which, in Britain at least,
have brought a heightened awareness of the implications of
racism and ethnic diversity.

In an article in *Feminist Review*[2] we have discussed some
of the ways in which the book would have benefited from a
clearer recognition that it was written by white British socialist-
feminists, drawing on our own experiences, and on analyses
that are often ethnocentric in their assumptions. While there
is a long and honourable tradition in feminism of producing
theory from our own experience and of political action in

---

[2] 'Ethnocentrism and Socialist-feminist Theory', *Feminist Review*, no. 20, 1985.
For responses see *Feminist Review* nos 22 & 23.

whatever patch we find ourselves in, it nevertheless was and is clearly not legitimate for white women to write as if those experiences are universal or that patch the whole field of struggle. Black women do not have access to this power of universalizing experiences, and it is a way in which white women within the feminist movement can and do use racial power and privilege. It is complicated for white women to negotiate this, of course, because the dominant voices in our society – those of the state, the media, the arts and so on – are those of their own dominating group. When we, as white individuals, react against the sexism that we have experienced or the family forms that we know best, we are reacting at the same time against the dominant ideology of the society, the traditions of Western art and so on. More important, it is these dominant ideas that also inform much of the state policy that affects everyone – the social security rules, the divorce laws, the tax regulations, the health service priorities. So it is all too easy for us to see society as having one homogeneously oppressive ideology.

There is a complex interplay between racism and ethnicity. In Britain racism has often been associated with immigration: with the idea that the Irish somehow 'belong' in Ireland, the Jews 'belong' in continental Europe, Asians in the Indian subcontinent or East Africa, Afro-Caribbeans in the Caribbean. 'British' culture is English culture, or at worst – the water gets a bit muddied here – Scots or Welsh; it is known, wholesome and homogeneous. It is usually cast as being unchanged since the days of Merrie England but *now* under threat from (in the nineteenth century) the Irish, (in the early twentieth century) the Jews, (in the mid to late twentieth century) immigrants from the Commonwealth. So the language of the more respectable racism has been that of a culture under threat and of cultural diversity. Racism has tended to exaggerate and stereotype cultural differences and to label them as 'ethnic' – that is to say as the traditions of a people, handed down from their ancestors and appropriate to that people.

Many anti-racists believe that the term 'ethnicity' should be avoided because it serves to mask racism: they argue that to attribute differential rates of imprisonment, disadvantage in the housing and labour markets, harassment in schools, beatings in the streets, fire-bombings of homes to ethnic difference or ethnocentrism is to play down and trivialize them. We would agree absolutely that racism and racial oppression must be named and exposed. But the problem is that cultural differences do exist and, indeed, develop in new ways and gain a new meaning in the context of racism.

The different cultures in Britain today are not 'ethnic' in the sense of being traditional cultures from different parts of the world transplanted to a new soil, whose only direction of change is likely to be towards assimilation with the dominant indigenous culture. They are, perhaps increasingly, cultures of resistance to racism and specific to the current economic and social position of the group concerned. For instance, the forms of Muslim belief, social organization and political mobilization in Britain are different from how they are in Pakistan or Bangladesh. Here, they are concerned with establishing community self-respect; with retaining the community allegiance of the younger generation; with claiming society-wide legal status and social recognition. Wearing traditional dress, celebrating traditional festivals, using *patois* or teaching children the mother tongue may often be articulated in traditional or conservative terms, but will often also incorporate a forward-looking strategy of personal resistance and community defence. What we have in Britain is a racialized form of ethnic diversity, which includes ethnic forms of resistance to racism.

So when Black feminists criticize the dominant white feminism, they say two things simultaneously: that we have ignored their experience of racism, privileging sexism as the major source of oppression; and that we have ignored ethnic difference and failed to see that their oppression *as women* may take very different forms from ours. These two are clearly distinct analytically but, because racism and ethnicity are so intertwined, in practice they are often indistinguishable. We wrote in *Feminist Review*, 'white feminism's racism takes the form of ethnocentrism in excluding the ethnically different views and experiences of black women.' With hindsight, and in the light of the debate that article engendered, we should have said that ethnocentrism is *one of* the forms that white women's racism has taken. An anti-racist feminism would not be simply one that was anti-racist as well as anti-sexist, but one that was acutely conscious at all times and in all contexts of who 'we', as political subjects, are.

What are the implications of all this when reading *The Antisocial Family*? Clearly, especially in Chapter II, many of the examples we have given, and some of the more detailed criticisms, are specific to the white family in Britain. What we wrote about relations between parents and children, for instance, or about romantic love and companionate marriage, drew on this specific experience. What we wrote about 'privacy as imprisonment' and the housewife's isolation in the nuclear family box is one among many possibilities for white women and may not correspond at all to the life of an Afro-Caribbean woman who works full time or an Asian woman who has women relatives living in the house or nearby. The ideology of the 'family wage' and the family dependent upon a male breadwinner may not exist as an ideal outside of the white working class, though it of course informs state policies on social security and on immigration and thus can impinge from the outside on everyone.

The fact that these particular criticisms do not apply to other family forms does not mean that they are not oppressive in different ways. In most societies, feminism has involved a fight against some aspects of the family: in India against dowry murders, in China against the ill-treatment of young brides by their husbands' families, in Ireland against the ostracism of unmarried mothers, in nineteenth-century England against the plight of spinsters, in contemporary Britain by Asian feminists against domestic violence. Most family systems have their bad side from the point of view of women, and family systems are invariably found as important structures of their oppression. So feminists in one society cannot adopt a cultural relativism which requires that they respect all the cultural patterns of another society. Feminists have to work towards forms of feminism that are prepared, where necessary, to be oppositional to any established culture.

'Deconstructing' the Family

In the third chapter we argued for a 'deconstructive' approach to the family (using the term loosely, rather than in the precise sense of deconstruction as a literary critical method). There is no such thing as *the* family which can be found in every society. The institutions that Western sociologists and anthropologists have labelled 'family' around the world have no essence that can be identified. There are, therefore, only particular types of domestic arrangement and kinship system which it may be convenient to call a type of family. The discussion of this theme was closely bound up in a critical consideration of Jacques Donzelot's *The Policing of Families*, since this book set out in a systematic way to treat the family not as an essentialist, unitary category but as an 'uncertain form whose intelligibility can only come from studying the system of relations it maintains with the socio-political level'. We put forward a number of criticisms of Donzelot's book, some of which have been seen as contentious, and stressed that the argument of *The Policing of Families* had an unfortunate anti-feminist slant to it. Indeed, one is tempted to add that it would be surprising if it had not, since in the foreword to the English translation Donzelot describes feminism (along with Marxism and psychoanalysis) as a form of discourse prone to 'certainties too repetitious to be credible'. Equally, we commented on the essentialist character of the family of the Ancien Régime as it appears in Donzelot, which reveals a failure to deconstruct and criticize the patriarchal family form as penetratingly as the modern, feminized variant. We would support this general line of argument still.

More complex, however, is the question of how to take the measure of the influence of Michel Foucault's ideas on feminist thought in the area of the family. *The Anti-social*

Family was in agreement with Donzelot's general theses in its inclination towards a deconstructive, anti-essentialist understanding of the history and social place of domestic and familial arrangements as well as in the weight attached to the familial construction of sociality. With the benefit of a decade's hindsight, it is perhaps now easier to consider the strands connecting these ideas on the family to the work of Foucault.

In all his work Foucault had relatively little to say about 'the family', just as he had little to say about other large constructs of the sociological mind, such as 'gender'. He had, however, a great deal to say about sexuality and sexual identities, about the historical construction of the body and about the importance of the political processes that produced subjugated subjects. Foucault's general concentration on marginality, in his work on crime, insanity and sexual identities, and his insistence on the importance of social processes that have little direct economic function but an enormous role in the general workings of power, are also significant in this context. He said in an interview:

> To put it very simply, psychiatric internment, the mental normalisation of individuals, and penal institutions have no doubt a fairly limited importance if one is only looking for their economic significance. On the other hand, they are undoubtedly essential to the general functioning of the wheels of power. So long as the posing of the question of power was kept subordinate to the economic instance and the system of interests which this served, there was a tendency to regard these problems as of small importance.[3]

Foucault's focus on the discursive construction of things by words, on the importance of what it is possible to say at a particular moment, is a perfect framework for looking at familialism as a discourse with normative powers.

Foucault's ideas have been taken up in feminism around

[3] Michel Foucault 'Truth and Power', in Colin Gordon, ed., *Power/Knowledge*, Brighton 1980, p. 116.

issues such as sexual identity and the social construction of sexed subjectivities and bodies. His arguments have been much more directly applicable there than in the attempt to rethink the unsatisfactory category of 'the family', with its ineradicable overtones of essentialism. The reverberation of Foucault's work on the study of 'the family' is thus rather indirect and negative – with the exception of Donzelot's book, by and large the influence of Foucauldian ideas has been to steer people away from entities such as 'the family'.

If one wanted proof of the constructedness of 'the family', one need look no further than the current debate about reproductive technology and parenthood. Since the introduction of artificial insemination, *in vitro* fertilization and its various applications, surrogate motherhood, and so on we have seen a major debate about the politics and ethics of these procedures and their implications for 'family life'. The debate as a whole, particularly the ease with which it is cast as a matter of family morality, illustrates some fascinating weaknesses of the naturalistic concept of the family. Technologies such as IVF, in which (in rare circumstances, admittedly) a previously infertile couple can have a child that belongs genetically to both of them, have a destabilizing effect on assumptions about parenthood and family. As Michelle Stanworth has argued, they have the paradoxical effect of undermining genetic parenthood at the same time as they pander to the desire for genetically related children.[4]

What has become crystal clear in these debates is how heavily conservative family morality has relied upon the appeal to what is 'natural'. Confronted with conceptions which are anything but natural, it does not know where to turn. Who, in the case of 'surrogate' motherhood, is the 'real' mother? The recognition that social can transcend biological maternity has escaped from the tolerated instance of adoption into a realm of evident public disquiet.

For sociologists and anthropologists, who understand bio-

---

[4] Michelle Stanworth, ed., *Reproductive Technologies: Gender, Motherhood and Medicine*, Cambridge 1987, Ch. 1.

logical reproduction in social terms, the situation is not so shocking. Various forms of surrogacy have long been practised, and the uniquely bonded mother and child is known to be a specific creation of the industrial middle class. The current rates of voluntary single motherhood are so high as to give the lie to the nuclear norm. More significantly, the rates of divorce and remarriage, and the very large rise in the number of 'reconstituted families', have altered for ever in Britain the relationship between adults and children: for many the relationship is one of voluntary social parenthood and the presumed norm of linked genetic, biological and social parenthood has been definitively ruptured. It will be interesting to see whether the forces of familism will regroup around a normative social image of the nuclear family irrespective of its genetic contents, or whether a more biologistic response occurs.

Familialism and the Politics of Personal Life

The Anti-social Family's main theme is the idea that while individual families may often approximate to an ideal of loving, caring and mutual aid and support, these values have only shallow roots elsewhere in the system as a whole. Privatized family collectivism tends to sap the strength of wider social collectivism. So the stronger and more supportive families are expected to be, the weaker the other supportive institutions outside of them become. Insofar as these other institutions are those of the state and of the locality, everyone in a given country is affected. Everyone who does not have the good fortune to be in a family that embodies the best of these supportive values is liable to find themselves isolated and socially impoverished. There may well be enclaves in which people manage to establish stronger forms of collectivism and solidarity. Some lesbians and gay men, for instance, have stronger bonds of mutual aid than their heterosexual urban peers. Indeed, the way in which gay men have collectively responded to the Aids crisis has given them the right to claim a title of 'community' with real substance to it. Embattled minority ethnic groups, too, often have stronger community organizations, whether religious or secular, and stronger networks of mutual aid. But none of this is a result of familialism, and familialism tends to weaken rather than enrich these forms of communality.

May 1991

Index

Printed in the United States
by Baker & Taylor Publisher Services